Selected Music
for Vespers

RECENT RESEARCHES IN MUSIC

A-R Editions publishes seven series of critical editions, spanning the history of Western music, American music, and oral traditions.

RECENT RESEARCHES IN THE MUSIC OF THE MIDDLE AGES AND EARLY RENAISSANCE
    Charles M. Atkinson, general editor

RECENT RESEARCHES IN THE MUSIC OF THE RENAISSANCE
    James Haar, general editor

RECENT RESEARCHES IN THE MUSIC OF THE BAROQUE ERA
    Christoph Wolff, general editor

RECENT RESEARCHES IN THE MUSIC OF THE CLASSICAL ERA
    Neal Zaslaw, general editor

RECENT RESEARCHES IN THE MUSIC OF THE NINETEENTH AND EARLY TWENTIETH CENTURIES
    Rufus Hallmark, general editor

RECENT RESEARCHES IN AMERICAN MUSIC
    John M. Graziano, general editor

RECENT RESEARCHES IN THE ORAL TRADITIONS OF MUSIC
    Philip V. Bohlman, general editor

Each edition in *Recent Researches* is devoted to works by a single composer or to a single genre. The content is chosen for its high quality and historical importance and is edited according to the scholarly standards that govern the making of all reliable editions.

For information on establishing a standing order to any of our series, or for editorial guidelines on submitting proposals, please contact:

A-R Editions, Inc.
Middleton, Wisconsin

800 736-0070 (North American book orders)
608 836-9000 (phone)
608 831-8200 (fax)
http://www.areditions.com

RECENT RESEARCHES IN THE MUSIC OF THE BAROQUE ERA, 161

Johann David Heinichen

Selected Music for Vespers

Edited by Margaret Williams

A-R Editions, Inc.
Middleton, Wisconsin

Performance parts are available from the publisher.

A-R Editions, Inc., Middleton, Wisconsin
© 2010 by A-R Editions, Inc.

All rights reserved. No part of this book may be reproduced or transmitted in any form by any electronic or mechanical means (including photocopying, recording, or information storage and retrieval) without permission in writing from the publisher.

The purchase of this edition does not convey the right to perform it in public, nor to make a recording of it for any purpose. Such permission must be obtained in advance from the publisher.

A-R Editions is pleased to support scholars and performers in their use of *Recent Researches* material for study or performance. Subscribers to any of the *Recent Researches* series, as well as patrons of subscribing institutions, are invited to apply for information about our "Copyright Sharing Policy."

Printed in the United States of America

ISBN-13: 978-0-89579-674-5
ISBN-10: 0-89579-674-0
ISSN: 0484-0828

♾ The paper used in this publication meets the minimum requirements of the American National Standard for Information Sciences—Permanence of Paper for Printed Library Materials, ANSI Z39.48-1992.

Contents

Acknowledgments   vii

Introduction   ix
   Heinichen's Biographers   ix
   Historical Background   ix
   The Composer   x
   The Dresden Court Musicians   xi
   The Music of the Edition   xi
   Notes on Performance   xii
   Notes   xiv

Plate   xvi

Psalms
   Beatus vir   3
   Confitebor tibi Domine   12
   Dixit Dominus   22
   In exitu Israel   40
      1. In exitu Israel   40
      2. Non nobis Domine   53
      3. Simulacra gentium   55
      4. Domus Israel   59
      5. Gloria   69
   Laetatus sum   72
   Lauda Jerusalem   84
   Laudate pueri   108
   Nisi Dominus   123

Magnificats
   Magnificat in G   135
      1. Magnificat   135
      2. Quia respexit   140
      3. Fecit potentiam   144
      4. Suscepit Israel   159
      5. Gloria   164
      6. Sicut erat in principio   165
   Magnificat in B-flat   176
      1. Magnificat   176
      2. Quia respexit   187
      3. Fecit potentiam   194
      4. Suscepit Israel   209
      5. Gloria   213

Hymns
    Ave maris stella   227
    Jesu Redemptor omnium   240

Marian Antiphons
    Alma Redemptoris Mater   255
    Ave Regina   269
        1. Ave Regina   269
        2. Gaude Virgo gloriosa   273
        3. Vale   278
    Regina caeli in G   284
        1. Regina caeli   284
        2. Quia quem meruisti   298
        3. Ora pro nobis   302
        4. Alleluia   307
    Regina caeli in D   317
        1. Regina caeli   317
        2. Quia quem meruisti   324
        3. Resurrexit sicut dixit   329
        4. Ora pro nobis   336
        5. Alleluia   337

Critical Report   347
    Sources   347
    Editorial Methods   350
    Critical Notes   351

Acknowledgments

The music in this volume is published by kind permission of Dr. Karl Wilhelm Geck and the Music Department of the Sächsische Landesbibliothek – Staats- und Universitätsbibliothek, Dresden. I thank Dr. Geck and all his staff for their unfailingly courteous and efficient help during my research visits to Dresden. I would also like to thank Dr. Janice B. Stockigt, of the University of Melbourne, for her encouragement and support during the course of my research, and for her generous sharing of her immense knowledge of the music of the Dresden court. I also acknowledge with gratitude the support and guidance of Dr. Glyn Jenkins of the University of Bristol. The initial research for this project was supported by funding from the Arts and Humanities Research Council.

Introduction

Heinichen's Biographers

The works presented in this volume comprise vespers music by Johann David Heinichen (1683–1729), author of one of the most important figured bass treatises of the baroque, *Der General-Bass in der Composition* of 1728.[1] Although known today mainly as a theorist, he was highly regarded in his own time as a composer, and for the last twelve years of his life held the prestigious position of *Kapellmeister* at the court of Friedrich August I in Dresden. There is a growing body of biographical writing on Heinichen, ranging in scope from Seibel's complete life-and-works study,[2] through surveys of particular genres,[3] to brief entries in general encyclopaedias. Many of the shorter biographical accounts share a strange characteristic. Writers dwell at some length on Heinichen's achievements as a composer of opera (despite fairly scanty information), and there is also an extensive description of *Der General-Bass in der Composition* in Walter's *Lexicon*,[4] but there is an almost complete lack of engagement with his work as a composer of church music, and even a lack of understanding of the nature of this repertoire. For example, Hiller, in his *Lebensbeschreibungen* (1784), damns him with faint praise, saying: "Heinichen's church music did not show the greatest fire; it was however also not dull."[5] He comments on the presence of fugues in any piece of particular length, and here he is a little more enthusiastic, saying they are a happy medium between being over and underworked. The entry on Heinichen in the *Allgemeine Encyclopädie der Wissenschaften und Künste* (1828) states that after 1720, "Heinichen only composed church music, mostly masses."[6] In his *Biographie Universelle* (1878), Fétis's only comment about the last years of his career was that "Heinichen's only task then was to direct the music of the court Catholic church."[7] His list of Heinichen's works, although fairly detailed about operatic compositions, is extremely limited in its description of church music, referring to the Dresden manuscripts as "several masses."[8] Even the *New Grove* entry is disappointing in its tally of Heinichen's church music, referring inaccurately to the vespers compositions as "35 Latin hymns and motets."[9] Finally, there is an extremely telling comment, made in passing by Buelow in his book *Thorough Bass Accompaniment According to Johann David Heinichen*. In his discussion of Heinichen's attitude towards counterpoint, Buelow writes: "One might think it strange, that Heinichen should bristle with such contempt for contrapuntists, when one sees the large number of church compositions in his catalogue of music."[10]

The assumptions, explicitly or implicitly running through all of this, are that if the object under discussion is church music, then we must for the most part be considering masses, and that the overriding compositional style—and certainly the only one worthy of any critical engagement—is counterpoint. However, as the music of this edition will show, the reality of Heinichen's church compositions and in particular his music for vespers is actually quite different, since the music embraces almost every possibility of the *stile moderno* available to composers of the first half of the eighteenth century.

Historical Background

In 1697, the Lutheran elector of Saxony Friedrich August I (also known as "August der Starke") was elected king of Poland, ruling there as August II. Although a shrewd political move, this assumption of the Polish crown by Friedrich August was not without its problems. One issue was distance. Dresden, the capital of Saxony, and the Polish capital of Warsaw are about 600 kilometers apart, and a corridor of land formed by the territories of Silesia and Brandenburg divided the two. But perhaps a more serious problem was that in order to assume the Polish crown, Friedrich August was obliged to convert to Catholicism.

This conversion horrified the Lutherans of Saxony. As Luther's birthplace, Saxony was the very cradle of the Reformation. Furthermore, as elector of Saxony, Friedrich August was, *ex officio*, the leader of the Corpus Evangelicorum, the body that since the Peace of Westphalia in 1648 had represented Protestant interests in the Habsburg Empire. The Saxon Lutherans sought assurances from the elector-king that their rights would be protected. They had particular reason to be fearful, since a ruling established at the Peace of Westphalia stipulated that "Cuius regnum eius religio"—that the state would follow the religion of its ruler. However, no attempt was made to force the Catholic faith on the Lutheran population, and the two faiths co-existed in Dresden, albeit sometimes uneasily. As well as being politically divisive, Friedrich August's conversion also had personal consequences.

His wife, Christiane Eberhardine of Brandenburg-Bayreuth, remained a Lutheran and moved away from Dresden after her husband's conversion.[11]

But Friedrich August had failed to convince Rome of the strength of his new Catholic faith. Following the Northern Wars and the 1706 Peace of Altranstädt (during which he lost, and then regained, the Polish crown), he decided to establish a proper Catholic court church. In order not to antagonize the Lutheran population, existing court buildings were used for the project, and in 1708 the new Catholic court church was opened, on a site that had previously been the court theater Am Taschenberg (see plate 1).[12]

A Jesuit mission was established in Dresden to run not only the new court church but also the Kapellknabeninstitut founded alongside the church. Initially the institute had ten pupils, boys and young men, referred to by the Jesuits as the "Juvenes," who were both singers and instrumentalists. The rules of the institute stated that the duties of the *Kapellknaben* were as follows:

> They will serve at the altar, read in turn at table, learn to sing figural music and to play instruments, study the Latin language, obey their teacher under the orders of the director.[13]

By the year of Heinichen's death, 1729, the number of *Kapellknaben* had risen to thirteen, and by 1731 there were seventeen.[14]

But still Rome was not satisfied. In 1710 the elector's only legitimate son, the electoral prince Friedrich August, had been confirmed in the Lutheran faith, as demanded by the marriage contract between Friedrich August I and Christiane Eberhardine. This confirmation drew a threatening letter from the pope,[15] and as a result the fifteen-year-old electoral prince was removed from the care of his mother and sent on a European grand tour. The prince's removal from his mother had the desired effect; his conversion to Catholicism took place in November 1712.[16]

This conversion was kept secret for several years. But by 1717 it was deemed necessary to make it public in order for Friedrich August I to achieve another of his political goals—the marriage of his son to the Habsburg princess Maria Josepha, elder daughter of the late emperor Joseph I. The wedding took place in Vienna in 1719, and when the couple returned to Dresden the festivities were long and lavish.[17]

The Dresden Jesuits were, not surprisingly, delighted with the arrival of Maria Josepha. Suddenly the Catholic court church achieved much prestige as the devout princess and her court introduced new feasts and extravagant ceremonials. This increasingly lavish setting was the context in which Heinichen composed his Catholic church music during the 1720s.

The Composer

Heinichen was born in Krössuln, near Weissenfels, on 17 April 1683. Like his father before him, he became a pupil at the Thomasschule in Leipzig, receiving instruction from the kantor Johann Kuhnau. On leaving the Thomasschule, Heinichen entered Leipzig University as a law student and after graduating in 1706 began a career as an advocate in Weissenfels.

Heinichen's legal career did not last long. He soon became involved in the musical life of the courts at Weissenfels, Zeitz, and Naumberg, and in 1709 he returned to Leipzig to compose for the opera house there. In 1710, Heinichen travelled to Italy, achieving some success as an opera composer in Venice. It was in Venice in 1716 that Heinichen met the electoral prince, who was then still on his grand tour. The prince engaged Heinichen as *Kapellmeister*, and Heinichen arrived in Dresden to take up his appointment at the beginning of 1717. He remained in Dresden until his death from tuberculosis on 16 July 1729.

Heinichen's Catholic church music was all composed during the last decade of his life, and it forms a substantial portion of his output.[18] The catalyst for this change of musical direction seems to have been an unpleasant scene that occurred in 1720, during a rehearsal for Heinichen's opera *Flavio Crispo*. Two of the Italian castrati singers employed by the court, Matteo Berselli and Francesco Bernardi, also known as Senesino, declared Heinichen's arias to be unsingable, and Senesino tore up a copy and threw it at Heinichen's feet.[19] Although Heinichen's handling of Italian texts can indeed be a little clumsy, circumstantial evidence does seem to suggest that this was a manufactured dispute, since the outcome was extremely convenient for several of those concerned. The elector immediately dismissed all the singers of the Italian opera company, thereby relieving himself of a heavy financial burden at a time of some economic difficulty. The two castrati, together with the soprano Marherita Durastanti, were able to leave Dresden and take up positions in Handel's opera company in London (Handel had been a visitor in Dresden the previous year). And Heinichen was obliged to turn his attention away from opera and concentrate instead on supplying music for the Catholic court church,[20] whose need for new music had increased considerably since the arrival of the princess Maria Josepha.

Few biographical details are known about this last decade of Heinichen's life. On 29 December 1721 in Weissenfels he was married to Erdmuthe Johanna Eubischen, and in 1723 the only child of the marriage, a daughter Erdmutha Friederika, was born.[21] The year 1728 saw the publication of his great theoretical work, *Der General-Bass in der Composition*.[22]

These details can be supplemented a little by a historical source that has only come to light relatively recently. In 1994, three volumes of a diary kept by the Jesuits who ran the Dresden mission were rediscovered, having been missing since World War II. The second of these volumes covers the years 1721–38 and has the title *Continuatio Diarij seu Protocolli a . . . FREDERICO AUGUSTO Dresdae in urbe sua Electorali institutae Societatis JESU Missionis. AB Anno 1721. usque ad Annum 1738, inclusive* (hereafter *Diarium*).[23] Heinichen's name appears regularly throughout the years 1721–29 (generally spelled as "Heiningen," occasionally "Heinigen"), mostly in entries reporting his compositions for the church, but occasionally too in other contexts. In August 1724, for example, Heinichen was invited by Fr. Hartmann, the author of the *Diarium* for that year, to listen to the audition of a new bass singer. A few days later, Heinichen went back to see Fr. Hartmann to express his reservations about the new singer and to suggest that a court messenger be taken on instead.[24] In 1725, Heinichen and some of the musicians employed at court accompanied the royal household on a pilgrimage to Pillnitz, causing Fr. Hartmann to remark that mass could not be sung in the Dresden church.[25] There are also hints of occasional discontent on the part of the *Kapellmeister*, as when the *Diarium* reports that Heinichen refused to produce any music in the absence of the princess Maria Josepha.[26]

The Dresden Court Musicians

It would be wrong to say that a single Hofkapelle was responsible for the music of the Catholic court church during the 1720s. There were in fact several groups of musicians involved in performing the church music of this time, and one of the issues for scholars in this field is to determine for which group particular works were intended.

The Kapellknabeninstitut has already been mentioned. Beginning as six singers and four instrumentalists in 1708, the annual reports from 1710 to 1715 show that the singers numbered 2–3 sopranos, 1–2 altos, and 1–2 tenors.[27] The Jesuit priests themselves acted as bass singers. The *Diarium* reports that in December 1722, a priest was brought to Dresden as a bass singer, because the royal family could no longer bear to listen to Fr. Jungwirth (the director of the *Kapellknaben* since 1709).[28]

It is thought that the *Kapellknaben* would have been responsible for singing the less demanding settings, although there is evidence that some of the young singers were extremely skilled. One such was the young Franz Benda, who as a boy sang as an alto with the Dresden *Kapellknaben*. His autobiography mentions the fact that Heinichen composed a setting of the *Regina caeli* for him.[29]

The other main group of musicians was known as the Royal Musicians (Regiis Musicis), comprising both singers and instrumentalists. The Royal Musicians were expected to perform in church as well as in the opera house. As described above, one group of Italian opera singers had all been dismissed in 1720. In 1725, a new group of Italians was engaged to perform at the court; these were the two female sopranos Margherita Ermini and Ludowica Seyfried, the castrati Andrea Ruota (soprano) and Nicolo Pozzi (alto), the tenor Matteo Luchini, and the bass Cosimo Ermini (husband of Margherita).[30] The male singers of this group would have performed in church.

Unlike the singers, the instrumentalists employed by the court at this time as Royal Musicians were a relatively stable group. Names that appear both in a list of 1719 and again in Jesuit records of 1729 are the *Concert-Meister* Jean Baptiste Volumier, the violinist Johann George Pisendel, the lutenist Silvius Leopold Weiss, Pantaleon Hebenstreit,[31] the bassist Jan Dismas Zelenka, the flautist Peter Gabriel Buffardin, and the oboist Johann Christian Richter.[32]

Other court employees seemed to join the musicians on an ad hoc basis; the court messenger who was used as a singer has already been mentioned, and the *Diarium* also notes other occasional players.[33] One further group of instrumentalists used in the court church consisted of the royal trumpets and drums (the Tubicines Regii), whose duties in the court church were to play *intraden* (an improvised tradition of fanfares) during important feasts, and to play as required in solemn liturgical music.[34] However, none of Heinichen's music for vespers requires the use of trumpets and drums.

Between the dismissal of the Italian opera singers in 1720 and the arrival of the new singers in 1725, it would appear that there were no virtuoso singers available to the court. Yet the *Diarium* during these years still describes music performed by the Royal Musicians. It is suggested that on these occasions the singers were supplied by a group of Italian comedy players (the Comici Italiani).[35] This group was directed by the Italian impresario Tommaso Ristori and his son Giovanni Alberto, and it is notable that from 1721, G. A. Ristori's name begins to appear in the *Diarium* as a composer of church music.

The Music of the Edition

Although a significant compositional duty for a *Kapellmeister* at a Catholic court was undoubtedly to compose settings of the mass, the composition of settings for the evening office of vespers was of nearly equal importance. Indeed, it might even be argued that settings for vespers offered composers significantly greater scope for expression, since unlike the ordinary of the mass, whose elements remain constant throughout the liturgical year, the components required for vespers vary.

The office begins with the versicle *Deus in adjutorum me intende*, followed by the respond *Dominus in adjuvandum me festina*. This is followed by five psalms, the first always *Dixit Dominus*, each with an associated antiphon that may come before or after the psalm, depending on local usage. The psalms are followed by a liturgical hymn and then the canticle (the Magnificat). When the following office of compline is not held, a Marian antiphon may then follow. The particular psalms to be sung (the formulae) differ from occasion to occasion, and there is also some local variation. The exact order of a Dresden vespers service is not certain; it is assumed, however, that the formulae used resembled those commonly in use, such as those described for the court in Vienna.[36] The items assembled in this volume are all the settings that would be required for two of the most common vespers formulae, Marian vespers and Sunday vespers. For Sunday vespers, the required psalms, numbered as in the Vulgate, are *Dixit Dominus* (109), *Confitebor tibi Domine* (110), *Beatus vir* (111), *Laudate pueri* (112), and *In exitu Israel* (113), and for Marian vespers the psalms are *Dixit Dominus* (109), *Laudate pueri* (112), *Laetatus sum* (121), *Nisi Dominus* (126), and *Lauda Jerusalem* (147).

TABLE 1
The Four-psalm Set of 1726

	Key	Meter & Tempo	Vocal Scoring	Instrumental Scoring
Laudate pueri	G major	¢ Allegro	SATB soli, SATB chorus	Oboes, strings, continuo
Laetatus sum	D major	3/8 Vivace	AT soli	2 horns, oboes, strings, continuo
Nisi Dominus	G minor	¢ Un poco Andante	SB soli	Solo oboe, strings, continuo
Lauda Jerusalem	D major	¢ Allegro	SATB soli, SATB chorus	2 horns, oboes, strings, continuo

Because of the variability of the musical requirements for the office of vespers, composers generally did not set the complete office as a single "work."[37] Instead, they composed sets or cycles of vespers music from which the appropriate elements could be selected as the need arose. For example, Heinichen's colleague Zelenka (1679–1745) gathered together thirty-three of his vespers settings (psalms and Magnificats) into a collection he called *Psalmi Vespertini totus anni*. He later assembled a second collection (called *Psalmi varii*) containing not only his own settings but also those of other composers.[38]

Heinichen's extant vespers settings held in Dresden comprise twenty-nine psalms (one in two versions), eight Magnificats (one in two versions), five Marian antiphons, and eight liturgical hymns (one of which is a parody). There are no settings by Heinichen of the opening versicle and respond, nor of any of the antiphons associated with the psalmody of the office. From the dates on the manuscripts, it can be seen that Heinichen often composed several items at a time for a particular feast, but on only one occasion does it seem that he composed all the requirements for a particular vespers service all at the same time.[39]

Heinichen uses a mixture of single and multi-movement settings. In general, psalms and hymns tend to be set as single movements, whereas Marian antiphons and the Magnificats tend to be set in several movements, although this is not an inviolable rule. Each item, be it in one or in several movements, is a self-contained, tonally closed unit. However, Heinichen did group together one set of four psalms, composed in December 1726, and these four are clearly intended to be performed together. The psalms in the set are *Laudate pueri*, *Laetatus sum*, *Nisi Dominus*, and *Lauda Jerusalem*,[40] and a note at the end of the *Laetatus sum* reads "Siegue [*sic*] Nisi Dominus," which (in this instance, at least) precludes the performance of an intervening antiphon. There are no thematic or motivic connections between the settings, but the group achieves a balance of keys, styles, and scoring (see table 1). There is also a strong "family resemblance" between the *Magnificat in G* and the *Regina caeli in G*, both composed in March 1727. As with the set of four psalms, there are no specific motivic connections, but the styles of the two are similar, and they share common details of orchestration, such as their treatment of the flutes.

Heinichen's musical style is characterized by the grace and elegance of his melodies and his imaginative orchestration. His vocal lines are easy-breathed and display typical *galant* poise. Movement between parts is often in thirds or sixths, and vocal phrases are often punctuated by short orchestral interjections, adding to a sense of periodicity. Particularly imaginative orchestrations in the settings in this volume include the third movement of the *Magnificat in B-flat* ("Fecit potentiam"), which is scored for two obbligato bassoons and two solo bass voices (as well as the usual strings, oboes, continuo, and SATB chorus), and the second movement of the *Regina caeli in G* ("Quia quem meruisti"), where a quartet of three oboes and bassoon, all *con sordini*, accompanies the solo tenor.[41] This Marian antiphon also uses flutes to striking effect in the first movement, where they are juxtaposed with unison strings in a manner reminiscent (or perhaps rather prescient) of the opening of J. S. Bach's *Christmas Oratorio*.[42]

Structurally, most of the movements of Heinichen's vespers settings are in ritornello form. As he discusses in *Der General-Bass in der Composition*, the harmonies he uses at the principal structural points remain within a well-defined ambitus of the starting key.[43] However, when the text demands, at particularly dramatic moments, Heinichen uses striking melodic motifs and bold harmonic progressions that move well away from the ambitus. Fugal movements occur in certain standard places, such as at the doxology (usually beginning at "Sicut erat in principio") in multi-movement settings, and all Heinichen's liturgical hymns are set contrapuntally, with *colla parte* instrumental parts. See table 2 for a list of the settings in this volume, their dates of composition (dates in parentheses are inferred, whereas the other dates are written in the sources), and keys.

Notes on Performance

Heinichen's standard orchestra comprised strings, oboes, and continuo (organ, violoncello, theorbo, bassoon, double bass[44]). To this, he sometimes added other instruments: horns, flutes, recorders, obbligato bassoons or oboes. The vocal choir is always in four parts (SATB), and there is generally only one soloist of each voice type. One of the very few exceptions is the "Fecit potentiam" movement of the B-flat *Magnificat* setting in this volume, which uses two solo basses.

The few sets of parts in Dresden show that the orchestra would have comprised 2–4 each of first and second violins, 2–4 violas, 2–4 violoncellos (some ripieno and some concertante), 1–2 double basses, organ, and theorbo.

TABLE 2
Summary of the Settings Contained in This Volume

	Date	Key
Psalms		
Beatus vir	May 1724	D minor
Confitebor tibi Domine	May 1727	A minor
Dixit Dominus	May 1724	B-flat major
In exitu Israel	(1722)	B-flat major
Laetatus sum	December 1726	D major
Lauda Jerusalem	December 1726	D major
Laudate pueri	December 1726	G major
Nisi Dominus	December 1726	G minor
Magnificats		
Magnificat	March 1727	G major
Magnificat	November 1728	B-flat major
Hymns		
Ave maris stella	November 1723	F major
Jesu Redemptor omnium	December 1724	F major
Marian Antiphons		
Alma Redemptoris Mater	(November 1723)	E-flat major
Ave Regina	March 1727	E-flat major
Regina caeli	March 1727	G major
Regina caeli	(1722)	D major

There are two oboe parts, and evidence from the scores suggests that two players played from each part. It also seems that (at least) two players played from the bassoon part. The vocal parts suggest a choir of 8–12 singers including the soloists, with the soloists also joining in the tutti choruses.

Oboes would have been expected as part of the instrumental ensemble for Heinichen's vespers music.[45] This can be inferred from a number of the autograph sources, which, although they contain no reference to oboes at the beginning of the score, do contain later reference to oboes in the form of instructions to copyists (e.g., the instruction "Hautb. tacet"). However, the most convincing evidence for the presence of oboes comes from a set of surviving parts to Heinichen's *Magnificat in F* (Dresden, Sächsische Landesbibliothek – Staats- und Universitätsbibliothek, shelf mark *D-Dlb* Mus. 2398-E-510). This *Magnificat* is Heinichen's own abridgement of his first *Magnificat in F* of 1721, and was made sometime in late 1723 or early 1724. The score of this abridged *Magnificat* (shelf mark *D-Dlb* Mus. 2398-D-22a) is completely silent about the inclusion of oboes; indeed, it contains no instrumental part names at all. However, the set of parts does include two for oboe.

As well as confirming the presence of oboes, this set of parts also shows the rules by which the Dresden oboe parts were constructed. As might be expected, oboe 1 doubles violin 1 and oboe 2 doubles violin 2, but the oboes fall silent during vocal solos, and are also silent during passages where the string parts are in unison and notated in the bass clef. Where Heinichen does include instructions on his scores about the oboes, it is in the cases when their use is contrary to this standard practice, as for example when he instructs that both oboes are to double the first violin.

Heinichen seemed to assume that his copyists would take a fair amount of responsibility for constructing the oboe parts. For example, a *Dixit Dominus* setting of 1727 includes a small sketch in a spare stave of the manuscript indicating the required rhythmic and melodic pattern of the oboe part, but the detail is left for the copyist to resolve. However, this faith in the copyists' abilities was not always entirely well placed. The copyists of the *Magnificat* parts described above went no further than to copy out verbatim the violin parts (although of course leaving the oboes out of the texture during vocal solos). This results in parts that, at times, fall well outside the normal compass of the oboe (going down to A below middle C on occasion), and also resulting in lines not particularly well suited to the instrument. It can only be assumed that the players would have taken on a fair degree of responsibility for adjusting their parts to be within range and to be suitable for their instruments' capabilities.

The players of the basso continuo line were organized into two groups: the concertante group who played throughout, and the ripieno group who, like the oboes, dropped out of the texture during solo vocal passages. The concertante group comprised the organ, theorbo, and violoncellos, and the ripieno group comprised bassoons, double basses, and (possibly) additional violoncellos. Having for convenience listed the bass instruments of this group as "double basses," it must be noted that the exact identity of this instrument is not clear. Instructions on the scores and the few separate part names refer to "Violoni," whereas court documents often mention players of the "Contrabass" (as, for example, Zelenka himself). It is possible that more than one type of instrument was involved.

This division of forces was used not only by Heinichen but also by his colleague Zelenka, and Zelenka was far more explicit in his scores, often including the instructions "tutti" or "solo" on the continuo line.[46] Heinichen's practice differs from Zelenka's in the matter of the continuo accompaniment to *stile antico* fugal movements where the continuo line is in the form of a *basso seguente*, following the lowest pitched vocal part. In both Heinichen's and Zelenka's work, the basso continuo line changes clef to match the lowest vocal part. However, where the lowest line is the tenor, Zelenka includes violoncello and theorbo in the continuo accompaniment, whereas Heinichen does not. In effect, this means that the normal arrangement for Heinichen's *stile antico* movements is that the organ is the only continuo instrument (playing either tasto solo, or with chordal realization, as indicated) unless the vocal basses are singing, in which case all the continuo instruments are used.

In this edition, the division of the forces of the continuo line is indicated by the use of the terms "Basso continuo" and "Basso ripieno." In *stile antico* fugal movements, the basso continuo is organ only, with all other instruments comprising the basso ripieno group. In all other movements, the basso continuo group is organ, violoncello, and theorbo, and the basso ripieno group comprises double bass, bassoon, and possibly additional violoncellos. Occasionally, as a special effect, Heinichen specifically requires a continuo grouping that differs somewhat from his usual practice; in this case, source instructions are included in the transcription.

Notes

1. Published in Dresden at the author's own expense. Available in facsimile reprint as *Der Generalbaß in der Komposition* (Hildesheim: Georg Olms Verlag, 1994).
2. Gustav Adolph Seibel, *Das Leben des Königl. Polnischen und Kurfürstl. Sächs. Hofkapellmeisters Johann David Heinichen nebst chronologischem Verzeichnis seiner Opern und thematischem Katalog seiner Werke* (Leipzig: Breitkopf & Härtel, 1913).
3. Eberhard Schmitz, "Die Messen Johann David Heinichens" (Ph.D. diss., University of Hamburg, 1967), for example.
4. Johann Gottfried Walther, *Musikalisches Lexikon oder Musikalische Bibliothek*, 1732 (facs. repr., Kassel: Bärenreiter, 1953), 306–7.
5. Johann Adam Hiller, *Lebensbeschreibungen berühmter Musikgelehrten und Tonkünstler neuerer Zeit* (Leipzig, 1784; facs. repr., Leipzig: Peters, 1979), 139.
6. Johann Samuel Ersch and Johann Gottfried Gruber, eds., *Allgemeine Encyclopädie der Wissenschaften und Künste*, part 2, vol. 4, ed. G. Hassel and U. G. Hoffman (Leipzig: Gleditsch, 1828), 195.
7. "Heinichen n'eut plus alors d'autre occupation que de diriger la chapelle catholique de la cour." François-Joseph Fétis, *Biographie universelle des musiciens et bibliographie générale de la musique* (Paris, 1878), 4:280.
8. Fétis, *Biographie universelle*, 4:280.
9. *The New Grove Dictionary of Music and Musicians*, 2nd ed., s.v. "Heinichen, Johann David" (p. 321), by George J. Buelow.
10. George J. Buelow, *Thorough-bass Accompaniment According to Johann David Heinichen* (Lincoln and London: University of Nebraska Press, 1986), 280.
11. She moved first to Torgau, then to Pretzsch. Wolfgang Horn, *Die Dresdner Hofkirchenmusik 1720–1745: Studien zu ihren Voraussetzungen ind ihren Repertoire* (Kassel: Bärenreiter, 1987), 21. It was on her death in 1727 that Bach wrote the *Trauerode*, BWV 198.
12. In fact, other Catholic chapels were also established in and around Dresden: a chapel in all but name in the hunting castle of Hubertusberg, a chapel in Leipzig in 1708, and a chapel in the Neustadt district of Dresden in 1739. See Janice Stockigt, *Jan Dismas Zelenka (1679–1745): A Bohemian Musician at the Court of Dresden* (Oxford: Oxford University Press, 2000), 27.
13. Horn, *Die Dresdner Hofkirchenmusik*, 36.
14. Stockigt, *Jan Dismas Zelenka*, 70.
15. See Horn, *Die Dresdner Hofkirchenmusik*, 22.
16. Siegfried Seifert, "Das *Diarium Missionis Societatis Jesu Dresdae ab anno 1710* als Quelle für Festordnung und Liturgie der der Dresdner katholischen Hofkirche," in *Zelenka-Studien II: Referate und Materialien der 2. Internationalen Fachkonferenz Jan Dismas Zelenka (Dresden und Prag 1995)*, ed. Günter Gattermann (Sankt Augustin: Academia Verlag, 1997), 30, is of the opinion that the conversion of the electoral prince arose out of religious conviction, rather than political necessity.
17. See the introductions to Johann David Heinichen, *La Gara degli Dei* and *Diana su l'Elba*, ed. Michael Walter, Recent Researches in the Music of the Baroque Era, vols. 102 and 103 (Madison, Wis.: A-R Editions, 2000).

18. For a complete list of Heinichen's works, see *Die Musik in Geschichte und Gegenwart*, 2nd ed., *Personenteil*, s.v. "Heinichen, Johann David" (cols. 1183–88), by Wolfgang Horn.
19. Moritz Fürstenau, *Zur Geschichte der Musik und des Theaters am Hofe zu Dresden* (Dresden, 1861; facs. repr., Hildesheim: Edition Peters, 1971), 2:153–54.
20. His first work for the Catholic court church, his *Missa Primitiva*, was composed for Pentecost, 1721.
21. Seibel, *Das Leben*, 24 and 25.
22. An earlier version of this treatise, entitled *Neu erfundene und Gründliche Anweisung . . . Zu . . . vollkommener Erlernung des General-Basses*, had been published in 1711.
23. Excerpts are published by Wolfgang Reich and Siegfried Seifert, "Exzerpte aus dem Diarium Missionis S. J. Dresdae," in *Zelenka-Studien II*, 315–75.
24. "Exzerpte aus dem Diarium Missionis S. J. Dresdae," 341. The *Diarium* does not report whether Heinichen's advice was followed.
25. "Exzerpte aus dem Diarium Missionis S. J. Dresdae," 343.
26. The entries for 2 and 5 December 1725. "Exzerpte aus dem Diarium Missionis S. J. Dresdae," 344–45.
27. Horn, *Die Dresdner Hofkirchenmusik*, 38.
28. "Exzerpte aus dem Diarium Missionis S. J. Dresdae," 337. The bass singer in Heinichen's vespers music often takes a somewhat priestly role. For example, the bass voice is often used to sing the beginning of the doxology ("Gloria Patri, et Filio, et Spiritui Sancto") when this is not set as a separate movement.
29. Paul Nettl, *Forgotten Musicians* (New York: Greenwood Press, 1951), 207. This might possibly be D-Dlb Mus. 2398-E-4.
30. Fürstenau, *Zur Geschichte*, 160. See also Stockigt, *Jan Dismas Zelenka*, 71.
31. Listed as "Cammer-Musicus," but known today mainly as the inventor of a dulcimer-like instrument named after him, the Pantaleon.
32. Fürstenau, *Zur Geschichte*, 134–37, and Stockigt, *Jan Dismas Zelenka*, 237–38. There may well have been more musicians employed on both dates, but Fürstenau's list does not give the names of all the rank and file players. Of the named musicians, Pisendel, Hebenstreit, Weiß, and Buffardin were still on the roster in 1746.
33. "Exzerpte aus dem Diarium Missionis S. J. Dresdae," 350. For example, the violinist Eiselt played on 3 November 1727.
34. See Ortrun Landmann, "The Dresden Hofkapelle during the Lifetime of Johann Sebastian Bach," *Early Music* 17 (1989): 23. This group was especially regarded as a symbol of the elector's high rank. Other court ensembles mentioned by Landmann, but not connected with the court church, were the so-called Polnische Kapelle (which accompanied the elector on his visits to Poland) and an ensemble of Jagdpfeiffers. The court also maintained a small Protestant Kapelle.
35. "Exzerpte aus dem Diarium Missionis S. J. Dresdae," 355. It is also possible that a similar group of French singers (the Galli Regii Musici) was occasionally used.

36. Whence Maria Josepha and her considerable retinue. See Wolfgang Horn and Thomas Kohlhase, *Zelenka-Dokumentation* (Wiesbaden: Breitkopf & Härtel, 1989), 1:119–20.

37. We have, perhaps erroneously, become used to regarding vespers collections such as the Monteverdi settings of 1610 as a complete work, rather than as a collection of separate elements, to be assembled as required.

38. Names in this collection included Caldara, Vivaldi, Brixi, and Poppe. The vespers music assembled for any one occasion could therefore contain settings by several different composers.

39. In May 1724, for the feast of Pentecost. Unfortunately, these cannot be offered as a complete set in publication, because the Marian antiphon, a setting of the *Regina caeli*, is now missing.

40. I.e., all the psalms except the opening *Dixit Dominus* that would be required for Marian vespers.

41. Janet K. Page, " 'To Soften the Sound of the Hoboy': The Muted Oboe in the 18th and Early 19th Centuries," *Early Music* 21 (1993): 65–80.

42. The model for this opening was of course the homage cantata *Tönet, ihr Pauken*, BWV 214, composed for the Dresden royal family.

43. The ambitus is defined in terms of steps around a musical circle. See Heinichen, *Der Generalbaß in der Komposition*, 837–916.

44. However, see below for discussion on the identity of the string bass instrument.

45. See Johann David Heinichen, *Magnificat in A*, ed. Wolfgang Horn (Stuttgart: Carus Verlag, 1986), iii–iv.

46. Thomas Kohlhase, "Anmerkungen zur Generalbaßpraxis der Dresdner Hofkirchenmusik der 1720er bis 1740er Jahre," in *Zelenka-Studien I: Referate der Internationalen Fachkonferenz J. D. Zelenka, Marburg, J.-G.-Herder-Institut, 16. – 20. November 1991*, ed. Thomas Kohlhase (Kassel: Bärenreiter, 1993), 233–40.

Plate 1. An engraving by Antoine Aveline (French engraver, 1691–1743) of a drawing by Raymond Leplat (1664–ca. 1743). Leplat was a court official and architect who worked with Mattheias Pöppelmann on the redesign of many court buildings. The plate depicts the ground floor of the Hofkapelle where the Heinichen works for vespers would have been first performed. This was the building that had once been the court theater Am Taschenberg. Copperplate engraving, reproduced by permission of the Staatliche Kunstsammlungen, Dresden. Photo: Rudolph Kramer, reproduced by permission of the SLUB Dresden / Deutsche Fotothek.

Psalms

Beatus vir

A solo
T solo
B.c.
vo- let ni- mis. Po- tens in ter- ra e- rit se- men e- jus: ge-ne-ra- ti-
-da- tis e- jus vo- let ni- mis. Po- tens in ter- ra e- rit se- men e- jus:
-o re- cto- rum be-ne- di- ce- tur. Glo- ri- a et di- vi- ti- ae in do- mo_ e- jus:
Glo- ri- a et di- vi- ti- ae in do- mo_ e- jus: et ju-
et ju- sti- ti- a e- jus_ ma- - net in sae- cu- lum sae- cu-
-sti- ti- a e- jus_ ma- - - net in sae- cu- lum sae- cu-
Fl. or Ob. 1
Fl. or Ob. 2
-li.
-li.
B.r.

22
mi- se- ri- cors, et mi- se- ra- tor, et
Ex- or- tum est in te- ne-bris lu- men re- ctis: mi- se- ri- cors, et mi- se- ra- tor, et
26
A solo
T solo
B.c.
ju- stus, mi- se- ri- cors, et mi- se- ra- tor, et ju- stus. Ju- cun- dus ho- mo qui
ju- stus, mi- se- ri- cors, et mi- se- ra- tor, et ju- stus. Ju-
29
mi- se- re- tur et com- mo- dat, dis- po- net ser-mo- nes su- os in ju- di- ci- o:
-cun- dus ho- mo qui mi- se- re- tur et com- mo-dat, dis- po- net ser-mo- nes su- os in ju- di- ci- o:
32
qui- a in ae- ter- num non com- mo- ve- bi- tur, non com-mo-
qui- a in ae- ter- num non com- mo- ve- bi- tur, non

35
Fl. or Ob. 1
Fl. or Ob. 2
A solo
-ve- bi- tur.
T solo
com- mo- ve- bi- tur.
B.r.
B.c.
38
41
ab au- di- ti- o- ne
In me- mo- ri- a ae- ter- na e- rit ju- stus:

44
A solo
ma- la non ti- me- bit. Pa- ra- tum cor e- jus spe- ra- re in Do- mi-
T solo
Pa- ra- tum cor e- jus spe- ra- re in Do- mi-
B.c.
47
-no, con- fir- ma- tum est cor e- jus: non com-mo- ve- bi-tur, non com-mo- ve-
-no, con- fir- ma-tum est cor e- jus: non com-mo- ve-
51
Fl. or Ob. 1
Fl. or Ob. 2
A solo
- bi- tur do- nec de- spi- ci- at i- ni- mi- cos su- os.
T solo
- bi- tur do- nec de- spi- ci- at i- ni- mi- cos su- os.
B.r.
B.c.
54
Di- sper- sit, di- sper- sit,
Di- sper- sit, di- sper- sit,

57
A solo
de- dit pau- pe- ri-bus: ju- sti- ti- a e- jus ma- net in
T solo
de- dit pau- pe- ri-bus: ju- sti- ti- a e- jus ma- net in
B.c.
7
60
sae- cu-lum sae- cu- li: cor- nu e- jus ex- al- ta- bi- tur in glo-
sae- cu-lum sae- cu- li: cor- nu e- jus ex- al- ta- bi- tur in glo-
[♯]
63
Fl. or Ob. 1
Fl. or Ob. 2
A solo
- ri- a.
T solo
- ri- a.
B.r.
B.c.
66
Pec- ca- tor vi- de- bit, et i- ra- sce- tur, et i- ra- sce- tur, pec- ca- tor vi-
Pec- ca- tor vi- de- bit, et i- ra- sce- tur, et i- ra- sce- tur, pec- ca- tor vi-
♯

69
A solo
-de- bit, et i- ra- sce- tur, et i- ra- sce- tur, den- ti- bus su- is fre- met, fre- met
T solo
-de- bit, et i- ra- sce- tur, et i- ra- sce- tur, den- ti- bus su- is fre- met, den- ti- bus su- is fre- met
B.c.
72
et ta- be- scet, ta- be- scet: de- si- de- - ri- um pec- ca- to- rum pe- ri- bit, pe-
et ta- be- scet, ta- be- scet: de- si- de- - ri- um pec- ca- to- rum pe- ri- bit, pe-
76
Fl. or Ob. 1
Fl. or Ob. 2
A solo
-ri- bit.
T solo
-ri- bit.
B.r.
B.c.
79
et Spi- ri- tu- i San- cto. Sic- ut
Glo- ri- a Pa- tri, et Fi- li- o, Sic- ut

83
e- rat in prin- ci- pi- o, et sem- per, sem- per, et in sae- cu- la sae- cu- lo- rum.
e- rat in prin- ci- pi- o, et sem- per, sem- per, et in sae- cu- la sae- cu-
86
A- men, a- men, a-
-lo- rum. A- men, a-
89
men, a- men,
men, a- men,

a- - men, a- men.

a- - men, a- men.

Confitebor tibi Domine

*For this setting, the basso ripieno comprises violoncello, theorbo, bassoon, and double bass.

9
-ni: ex- qui- si- ta in om- nes vo- lun- ta- tes e- jus. Con- fes- si- o et ma- gni- fi-
-ni: ex- qui- si- ta in om- nes vo- lun- ta- - tes e- jus. Con- fes- si- o
-ni: ex- qui- si- ta in om- nes vo- lun- ta- tes e- jus.
-ni: ex- qui- si- ta in om- nes vo- lun- ta- tes e- jus.
[tasto solo]
13
-cen- ti- a o- pus e- jus: et ju- sti- ti- a e- jus ma- net in sae- cu- lum
et ma- gni- fi- cen- ti- a o- pus e- jus: et ju- sti- ti- a e- jus ma- net in
et ju- sti- ti- a e- jus ma- net, ma- net in sae- cu- lum
ma- net in sae- cu- lum
[7]

17
sae- cu- li. mi- se- ri-
sae- cu- lum sae- cu- li. mi- se- ri- cors et
sae- cu- li. Me- mo- ri- am fe- cit mi- ra- bi- li- um su- o- rum, mi-
sae- cu- li. Me- mo- ri- am fe- cit mi- ra- bi- li- um su- o- rum, mi- se- ri-
21
-cors et mi- se- ra- tor Do- mi- nus: e- scam de- dit ti-
mi- se- ra- tor Do- mi- nus: e- scam de- dit ti-
-se- ri- cors et mi- se- ra- tor Do- mi- nus: e- scam de- dit ti-
-cors et mi- se- ra- tor Do- mi- nus: e- scam de- dit ti-

-mentibus se. Memor erit in saeculum testamenti -mentibus se. Memor erit in saeculum testamenti sui -mentibus se. Memor erit in saeculum testamenti -mentibus se.

sui: virtutem operum suorum annuntiabit populo
sui: virtutem operum suorum annuntiabit po-
virtutem operum suorum annuntiabit

33
Ut det il- lis hae- re- di- ta- tem gen- ti- um:
su- o: Ut det il- lis hae- re- di- ta- tem gen- ti- um:
- pu- lo su- o: o- pe- ra ma- nu- um e- jus
po- pu- lo su- o: o- pe- ra ma- nu- um e- jus
[tasto solo]
[5]
37
Fi- de- li- a om- ni- a man- da- ta
ve- ri- tas et ju- di- ci- um. Fi- de- li- a om- ni- a man- da- ta
ve- ri- tas et ju- di- ci- um. Fi- de- li- a om- ni- a man- da- ta
ve- ri- tas et ju- di- ci- um. Fi- de- li- a om- ni- a man- da- ta
[♯6]
[♯6]

e- jus: con- fir- ma- ta in sae- cu- lum sae- cu- li: fa- cta in
e- jus: con- fir- ma- ta in sae- cu- lum sae- cu- li: fa- cta in
e- jus: con- fir- ma- ta in sae- cu- lum sae- cu- li: fa- cta in
e- jus: con- fir- ma- ta in sae- cu- lum sae- cu- li: fa- cta in

[7 6 #]   [#]

ve- ri- ta- te et ae- qui- ta- te.
ve- ri- ta- te et ae- qui- ta- te. Re- dem- pti- o- nem
ve- ri- ta- te et ae- qui- ta- te. Re- dem- pti- o- nem mi- sit
ve- ri- ta- te et ae- qui- ta- te.

[tasto solo]

49
man- da- vit in ae- ter- num te- sta-men- tum su-
mi- sit po- pu- lo su- o: man- da- vit in ae- ter- num te- sta- men- tum su-
po- pu- lo su- o: man- da- vit in ae- ter- num te- sta- men- tum su-
man- da- vit in ae- ter- num te- sta- men- tum su-
[5]
53
-um. San- ctum et ter- ri- bi- le no- men e- jus: i-
-um. San- ctum et ter- ri- bi- le no- men e- jus: i-
-um. San- ctum et ter- ri- bi- le no- men e- jus: i-
-um. San- ctum et ter- ri- bi- le no- men e- jus:
[6 4 ♯2]
[♯]

57
-ni- ti- um sa- pi- en- ti- ae ti- mor Do- mi- ni. In- tel- le- ctus
-ni- ti- um sa- pi- en- ti- ae ti- mor Do- mi- ni. In- tel-
ni ti um sa pi en ti ae ti mor, ti- mor Do- mi- ni.
i- ni- ti- um sa- pi- en- ti- ae ti- mor Do- mi- ni.
[tasto solo]
61
bo- nus om- ni- bus fa- ci- en- ti- bus e- um:
-le- ctus bo- nus om- ni- bus fa- ci- en- ti- bus e- um: lau- da- ti- o e- jus
lau- da- ti- o e- jus ma- net in
lau- da- ti- o e- jus ma- net in
[5]
[♯]

Gloria Patri, gloria Filio, gloria et Spiritui Sancto. Sicut erat in principio

manet. Gloria Patri, gloria Filio, gloria et Spiritui Sancto. Sicut erat, sicut

saeculum saeculi. Gloria Patri, gloria Filio, gloria et Spiritui Sancto.

saeculum saeculi. Gloria Patri, gloria Filio, gloria et Spiritui Sancto.

75
-ci- pi- o, et nunc, et nunc, et sem- per, et in sae- cu- la
e- rat in prin- ci- pi- o, et in sae- cu- la sae- cu-
et in sae- cu- la sae- cu- lo- rum. A- men,
et in sae- cu- la sae- cu- lo- rum. A-
79
sae- cu- lo- rum. A- men, a- men, a- men.
-lo- rum. A- - men, a- - men.
a- men, a- men, a- - - men.
- men, a- men, a- - men.
[♯]

Dixit Dominus

9
Ob. 1
Ob. 2
Vn. 1
Vn. 2
Va.
S
A
T
B
B.r.
B.c.
p
p
p
Di- xit Do- mi-nus Do- mi- no me- o, di- xit:
Di- xit Do- mi-nus Do- mi- no me- o, di- xit:
Di- xit Do- mi-nus Do- mi- no me- o, di- xit:
solo
Di- xit Do- mi-nus Do- mi- no me- o, di- xit: Se- de a
13
de- xtris me- is. Do-nec po- nam i- ni- mi-cos tu- os, do- nec po- nam i-

- ni- mi- cos tu- os, i- - ni- mi- cos tu- os, sca- bel- lum__ pe- dum tu- o- rum.

Vir- gam vir-tu- tis tu- ae e- mit- tet, e- mit- tet Do- mi- nus ex Si-

-on: do-mi-na- re [in] me- di-o i- ni-mi- co- rum, i- ni-mi-co- rum tu- o- rum, tu-

-on: do- mi- na- re in me- di- o i- ni-mi-co- rum

-on: do- mi-na- re in me- di- o i- ni-mi-co- rum, i- ni- mi-

-on: do- mi- na- re in me- di- o i- ni- mi- co-

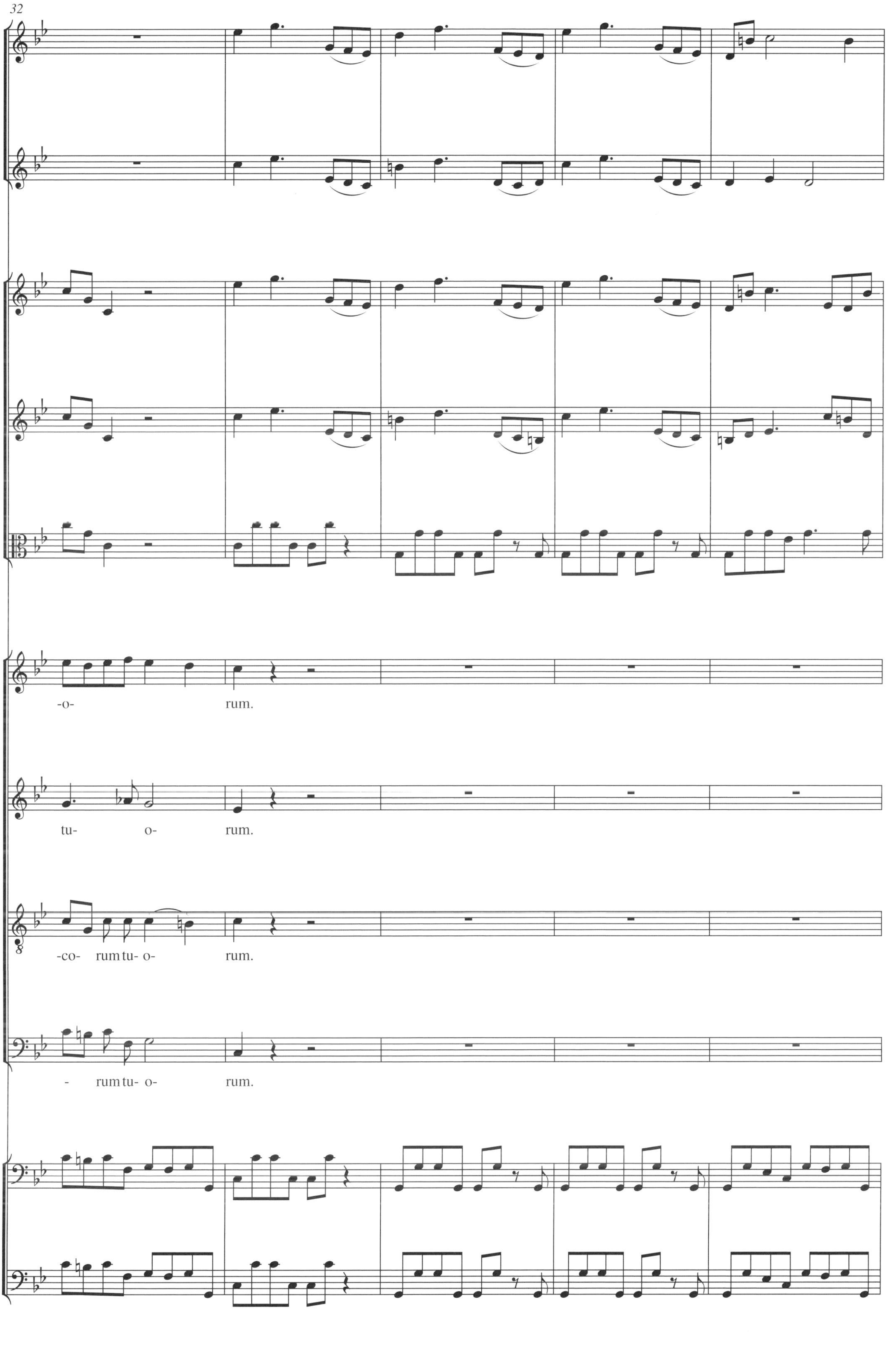
32
-o- rum.
tu- o- rum.
-co- rum tu- o- rum.
- rum tu- o- rum.

28

49
Vn. 1
Vn. 2
T
pae- ni- te- bit e- um: Tu es sa- cer- dos in ae- ter-
B.c.
53
- num se- cun- dum or- di- nem, se- cun- dum or- di-
57
Ob. 1
Ob. 2
Va.
S
[tutti]
Do- mi- nus a de- xtris tu- is, con- fre- git in
A
[tutti]
Do- mi- nus a de- xtris tu- is, con- fre- git in
tutti
-nem Mel- chi- - se-dech. Do- mi- nus a de- xtris tu- is, con-
B
tutti
Do- mi- nus a de- xtris tu- is, con-
B.r.

61
di- e i- rae su- ae re- ges. Ju- di- ca- bit, ju- di- ca- bit in na- ti-
di- e i- rae su- ae re- ges. Ju- di- ca- bit in na- ti- o- ni-
-fre- git in di- e i- rae su- ae re- ges. Ju- di- ca- bit in na- ti- o- ni-
-fre- git in di- e i- rae su- ae re- ges. Ju- di- ca- bit in na- ti- o- ni-bus,

65
-o- ni- bus, im- ple- bit ru- i- nas: con-quas-sa- bit
-bus, im- ple- bit ru- i- nas, im- ple- bit ru- i- nas: con- quas-
-bus, im- ple- bit ru- i- nas, im- ple- bit ru- i- nas: con-quas-
im- ple- bit ru- i- nas, im- ple- bit ru- i- nas: con-quas-

68
ca- pi- ta in ter- ra mul- to- rum. De tor- ren- te in vi- a
-sa- bit ca- pi- ta in ter- ra mul- to- rum. De tor- ren- te in
-sa- bit ca- pi- ta in ter- ra mul- to- rum. De tor- ren- te in
-sa- bit ca- pi- ta in ter- ra mul- to- rum. De tor- ren- te in

71
bi- bet: pro- pte- - re- a ex- al- ta- bit ca-
vi- a bi- bet: pro- pte- re- a ex- al- ta- bit ca-
vi- a bi- bet: pro- pte- re- a ex- al- ta- bit ca-
vi- a bi- bet: pro- pte- re- a ex- al- ta- bit ca-

74
-put.
-put.
-put.
-put.
à 3
[à 3]
[à 3]
Glo- ri- a
Glo- ri- a
Glo- ri- a
79
S
A
T
B.c.
Pa- tri, et Fi- li- o, et Spi- ri- tu- i
Pa- tri, et Fi- li- o, et Spi-
Pa- tri, et Fi- li- o, et Spi-

35

95
Ob. 1
Ob. 2
Vn. 1
Vn. 2
Va.
S
[tutti]
Sic- ut e- rat in prin- ci- pi- o, et nunc, et sem- per, et in sae- cu- la
A
[tutti]
Sic- ut e- rat in prin- ci- pi- o, et nunc, et sem- per, et in sae- cu-
T
[tutti]
Sic- ut e- rat in prin- ci- pi- o, et nunc, et sem- per, et in sae- cu-
B
tutti
-men, sic- ut e- rat in prin- ci- pi- o, et nunc, et sem- per, et in sae- cu- la
B.r.
B.c.

37

103
a- men, et in sae- cu-la sae-cu- lo-rum, a- men, et in sae- cu-
a- men, et in sae- cu-la sae-cu- lo-rum, a- men, a- men, et in sae- cu-
a- men, a- men, et in sae- cu-la sae-cu- lo-rum, a- men, a- men, et in
- men, et in sae- cu-la sae-cu- lo-rum, a-men, a- men, et in

107
-la sae-cu- lo- rum, a- men, a- men, a- men, a- - men.
-la sae-cu- lo- rum, a- men, a- men, a- - men.
sae- cu- la sae- cu- lo- rum, a- men, a- men, [a- men.]
sae- cu- la sae- cu- lo- rum, a- - men.

In exitu Israel

1. In exitu Israel

5
S
ex- i- tu Is- ra- el de Ae- gy- pto, do- mus
A
Ae- gy- pto, de Ae- gy- pto, do- mus Ja- cob de po- pu- lo
T
ex- - i- tu Is- - ra- el de Ae- gy- pto,
B
In ex- i- tu Is- ra- el de Ae- gy- pto,
Vc.
Bn.
Org.
Tbo.
D.b.
9
Ja- cob de po- - pu- lo bar- - ba- ro. Fa- cta
bar- ba- ro Fa- cta est Ju- dae- a san- cti- ti- ca- ti- o
do- mus Ja- cob de po- pu- lo bar- ba- ro. Fa- cta est Ju- dae- a san-
do- mus Ja- cob de po- pu- lo bar- ba- ro. Fa- cta est Ju-

42

21
fu- git, et fu- git, ma- re vi- dit, et fu- git, et fu- git: Jor-
24
-da- nis con- ver- sus est re- tror- sum, Jor- da- nis con- ver- sus est re-

44

31
a- gni, sic- ut a- gni o- vi-um. Quid est ti- bi ma- re
a- gni, sic- ut a- gni o- vi-um. Quid
a- gni, sic- ut a- gni o- vi-um. Quid est ti- bi
a- gni, sic- ut a- gni o- vi-um.

46

40
Ob. 1
Ob. 2
Vn. 1
Vn. 2
Va.
S
et tu Jor- da- nis, qui- a con- ver- sus es re- tror- sum?
A
et tu Jor- da- nis, qui- a con- ver- sus es re- tror- sum?
T
et tu Jor- da- nis, qui- a con- ver- sus es re- tror- sum?
B
-gi- sti? et tu Jor- da- nis, qui- a con- ver- sus es re- tror- sum?
Vc.
Bn.
Org.
Tbo.
D.b.

Montes exsultastis, exsultastis sicut a-

-ri- e- tes, et col- les sic- ut, sic- ut a- gni o- vi- um?

49
Vn. 1
Vn. 2
Va.
S
A fa- ci- e Do- mi-ni mo- ta est ter- ra,
A
A fa- ci- e Do- mi-ni mo- ta est ter- ra,
T
A fa- ci- e Do- mi-ni mo- ta est ter- ra,
B
A fa- ci- e Do- mi-ni mo- ta est ter- ra,
Vc.
Bn.
Org.
Tbo.
D.b.
6
4

52
a fa- ci- e Do- mi-ni mo- ta est ter- ra,
a fa- ci- e Do- mi-ni mo- ta est ter- ra,
a fa- ci- e Do- mi-ni mo- ta est ter- ra,
a fa- ci- e Do- mi-ni mo- ta est ter- ra,
6
4

mo- ta est ter- ra, a fa- ci- e De- i Ja- cob: Qui con-
vertit petram, petram in stagna aquarum, et rupem in

61
fon- tes a- qua- - -
ru- pem in fon- tes a- qua- -
fon- tes a- qua- - -
ru- pem in fon- tes a- qua- -
[♮]

64
- rum, et ru- pem in fon- tes a- qua- rum, a-
- rum, et ru- pem in fon- tes a- qua- rum, a-
- rum, et ru- pem in fon- tes a- qua- rum, a-
- rum, et ru- pem in fon- tes a- qua- rum, a-

2. Non nobis Domine

11
ve- ri- te tu- a: ne- quan- do di- cant gen- tes:
ve- ri- te tu- a: ne- quan- do di- cant, quan- do di- cant gen- tes:
ve- ri- te tu- a: ne- quan- do di- cant gen- tes, gen- tes:
16
U- bi est De- us e- o- rum? De- us au- tem no- ster in cae-
U- bi est De- us e- o- rum? De- us au- tem no- ster in cae-
U- bi est De- us e- o- rum? De- us au- tem no- ster in cae-
22
-lo: om- ni- a, om- ni- a quae- cum- que vo- lu- it, fe-
-lo: om- ni- a, om- ni- a quae- cum- que vo- lu- it, fe-
-lo: om- ni- a, om- ni- a quae- cum- que vo- lu- it, fe-
7
♯
28
-cit, fe- - - - - cit.
-cit, fe- - - cit, fe- cit.
-cit, quae- cum- que vo- lu- it, fe- cit, fe- - cit.
[♯]

3. Simulacra gentium

4
Vn. 1
Vn. 2
Va.
S
A
T
B
B.c.
à 3
et non lo-quen-tur: et non vi- de- bunt. et non au- di-ent:
[à 3]
et non lo-quen-tur: et non vi- de- bunt. et non au- di-ent:
[à 3]
et non lo-quen-tur: et non vi- de- bunt. et non au- di-ent:
ha- bent, o- cu-los ha- bent, Au- res ha- bent, na- res

7
et non o- do- ra- bunt. et non pal- pa- bunt: et non am-bu- la- bunt: non cla-
et non o- do- ra- bunt. et non pal- pa- bunt: et non am-bu- la- bunt: non cla-
et non o- do- ra- bunt. et non pal- pa- bunt: et non am-bu- la- bunt: non cla-
ha- bent, Ma- nus ha- bent, pe- des ha- bent,

10
Ob. 1
Ob. 2
Vn. 1
Vn. 2
Va.
S
tutti
-ma- bunt, non cla- ma- bunt [in gut- tu- re su- o.] Si- mi- les il- lis fi- ant qui fa- ci-unt e- a: et om- nes qui con-
A
tutti
-ma- bunt, non cla- ma- bunt [in gut- tu- re su- o.] Si- mi- les il- lis fi- ant qui fa- ci-unt e- a: et om- nes qui con-
T
tutti
-ma- bunt, non cla- ma- bunt [in gut- tu- re su- o.] Si- mi- les il- lis fi- ant qui fa- ci-unt e- a: et om- nes qui con-
B
tutti
Si- mi- les il- lis fi- ant qui fa- ci-unt e- a: et om- nes qui con-
B.r.
B.c.
7
♮
7
6

-fi- dunt in e- is, qui con- fi- dunt, qui con- fi- dunt in e- is.

-fi- dunt in e- is, qui con- fi- dunt, qui con- fi- dunt in e- is.

-fi- dunt in e- is, qui con- fi- dunt, qui con- fi- dunt in e- is.

-fi- dunt in e- is, qui con- fi- dunt, qui con- fi- dunt in e- is.

4. Domus Israel

60

21
Do- mus A- a-ron spe- ra- vit in Do- mi- no: ad- ju- tor e-
27
f
p
-o- rum et pro- te- ctor e- o- rum est. Qui ti-ment

Vn. 1
Vn. 2
S solo
B.c.
Do- mi-num spe-ra- ve- runt in e- um: ad- ju- tor e-
-o- rum et pro- te- ctor e- o- rum est. Do- mi-nus me- mor fu- it
no- stri: et be- ne- di- xit no- bis. Be- ne- di- xit
do- mu- i Is- ra-el: be- ne- di- xit do- mu- i Aa- ron.

54
Be-ne- di- xit om- ni-bus qui ti- ment Do- mi-num, pu-sil- lis
60
Ob. 1
Ob. 2
Vn. 1
Vn. 2
Va.
S solo
cum ma- jo- - ri- bus.
B.r.
B.c.
f
65
p
f

70
Ob. 1
Ob. 2
Vn. 1
Vn. 2
Va.
T solo
B.r.
B.c.
Ad- ji- ci- at Do- mi- nus su- per vos: su- per vos, et fi- li- os
76
f
ve- stros. Be- ne- di- cti vos a Do- mi- no,

81
Vn. 1
Vn. 2
T solo
B.c.
p
p
qui fe- cit cae- lum et ter- ram. Cae- lum
7 6
86
cae- li Do- mi- no: ter- ram autem de- dit fi- li- is
91
Ob. 1
Ob. 2
Vn. 1
Vn. 2
Va.
T solo
B.r.
B.c.
f
ho- mi- num.

96
Ob. 1
Ob. 2
Vn. 1
Vn. 2
Va.
B solo
B.r.
B.c.
p
Non mor- tu- i lau- da- bunt, lau- da- bunt te Do- mi- ne:
101
ne- que om- nes qui de- scen- -
105
- dunt in in- fer- num. Sed nos qui vi- vi- mus, be- ne- di- ci-mus

111
Do- mi- no, be- ne- di- ci-mus Do- -
116
- - - mi-no, ex hoc nunc et u- sque in
121
Ob. 1
Ob. 2
Vn. 1
Vn. 2
Va.
B solo
sae- - - cu- lum.
B.r.
B.c.

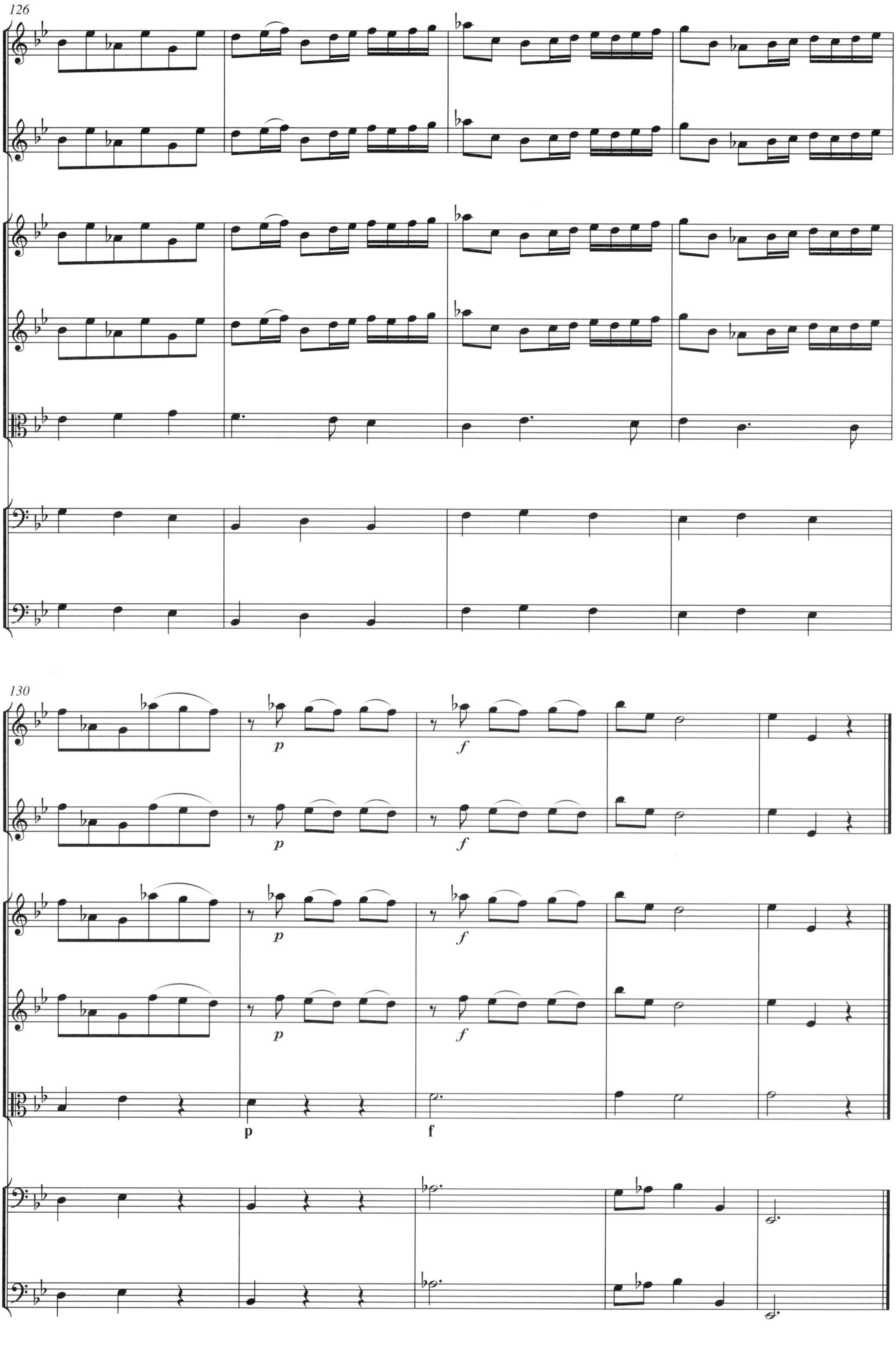
126
Ob. 1
Ob. 2
Vn. 1
Vn. 2
Va.
B.r.
B.c.
130
p
f
p
f
p
f
p
f
p
f

5. Gloria

8
-rum, a- men, a- men, a- men, a- - men, a-
-lo- rum, a- men, a- - men, a- men, a- men, a- men, a- men,
et in sae- cu- la sae- cu- lo- rum, sae- cu- lo- - rum, a- men, a- men,
et in sae- cu- la sae- cu- lo-rum, a- men, a- men,

11
- men, a- men, et in sae- cu- la sae- cu- lo-
a- men, a- men, et in sae- cu- la sae- cu- lo- rum, a-
a- men, et in sae- cu- la sae- cu-
a- men, a- men,

71

Laetatus sum

11
Hn. 1
Hn. 2
Ob. 1
Ob. 2
Vn. 1
Vn. 2
Va.
A solo
Lae-
T solo
Lae- ta-
B.r.
B.c.
17
A solo
-ta- - tus, lae- ta- tus sum in his quae di- cta sunt
T solo
- tus, lae- ta- tus sum in his quae di- cta sunt
6 6 4 5 3
B.c.
23
mi- hi: In do- mum Do- mi- ni i- bi- mus. Stan- tes
mi- hi: In do- mum Do- mi- ni i- bi- mus.

30
e- rant pe- des, pe- des no- stri, in a- tri- is
Stan- tes e- rant pe- des no- - stri, in a- tri- is tu-
37
Hn. 1
Hn. 2
Ob. 1
Ob. 2
Vn. 1
Vn. 2
A solo
tu- is Je- ru- sa- lem.
T solo
-is Je- ru- sa- lem.
B.r.
B.c.

75

63
A solo
Is- ra- el ad con- fi- ten- dum no- mi- ni Do- mi- ni. Qui- a
T solo
Qui- a il- lic se-
B.c.
70
il- lic se- de- runt se- des in ju- di- ci- o,
-de- runt, se- de- runt se- des in ju- di- ci- o, se- des
77
Hn. 1
Hn. 2
Ob. 1
Ob. 2
Vn. 1
Vn. 2
Va.
f
se- des su- per do- mum Da- vid.
su- per do- mum Da- vid.
B.r.
B.c.

83
Hn. 1
Hn. 2
Ob. 1
Ob. 2
Vn. 1
Vn. 2
Va.
T solo
Ro- ga- - te quae ad pa- cem
B.r.
B.c.
90
A solo
et a- bun- dan- ti- a di- li- gen- ti- bus te Fi- at
T solo
sunt Je- ru- sa- lem: Fi- at
B.c.
97
Hn. 1
Hn. 2
A solo
pax, pax, pax in vir- tu- te tu- a: et a- bun- dan- ti- a in
T solo
pax, pax, pax in vir- tu- te tu- a: et a- bun- dan- ti- a in
B.c.

104
Hn. 1
Hn. 2
Ob. 1
Ob. 2
Vn. 1
Vn. 2
Va.
A solo
tur- ri- bus tu- is. Pro- pter fra- tres me- os et pro- xi- mos
T solo
tur- ri- bus tu- is.
B.r.
B.c.
111
Vn. 1
p
Vn. 2
p
Va.
p
A solo
me- os, lo- que- bar pa- cem de te:
T solo
Pro- pter do- mum
B.c.

117
A solo
Pro- pter do- mum Do- mi- ni De- i no- stri, quae-
T solo
Do- mi- ni De- i no- stri, quae- si- vi bo-
B.c.
124
Hn. 1
Hn. 2
Ob. 1
Ob. 2
Vn. 1
f
Vn. 2
f
Va.
f
A solo
-si- vi bo- na ti- bi.
T solo
-na ti- bi.
B.r.
B.c.

Gloria Patri, gloria Filio, gloria et Spiritui Sancto. Sicut erat in principio, et

144
Hn. 1
Hn. 2
Ob. 1
Ob. 2
Vn. 1
Vn. 2
Va.
A solo
nunc, et sem- per, sem- per, et in sae- cu- la
T solo
[nunc, et sem- per, sem- per,] et in
B.r.
B.c.
151
A solo
sae- cu- lo- rum, a- - - - men,
T solo
sae- cu- la sae- cu- lo- rum, a- - men,
B.c.

157
Hn. 1
Hn. 2
Vn. 1
p
Vn. 2
p
A solo
a- - - - men,
T solo
a- men, a- - -
B.c.
164
A solo
et in sae- cu- la sae- cu- lo- rum, a- - -
T solo
- men, et in sae- cu- la sae- cu- lo- rum, a- -
B.c.
7
6
4
171
Hn. 1
Hn. 2
A solo
- - - men, a- men, a- men,
T solo
- - - men, a- men, a- men,
B.c.

177
Hn. 1
Hn. 2
Vn. 1
Vn. 2
Va.
A solo
a- - men.
T solo
a- - men.
B.r.
B.c.
184
Hn. 1
Hn. 2
Ob. 1
Ob. 2
Vn. 1
Vn. 2
Va.
B.r.
B.c.

Lauda Jerusalem

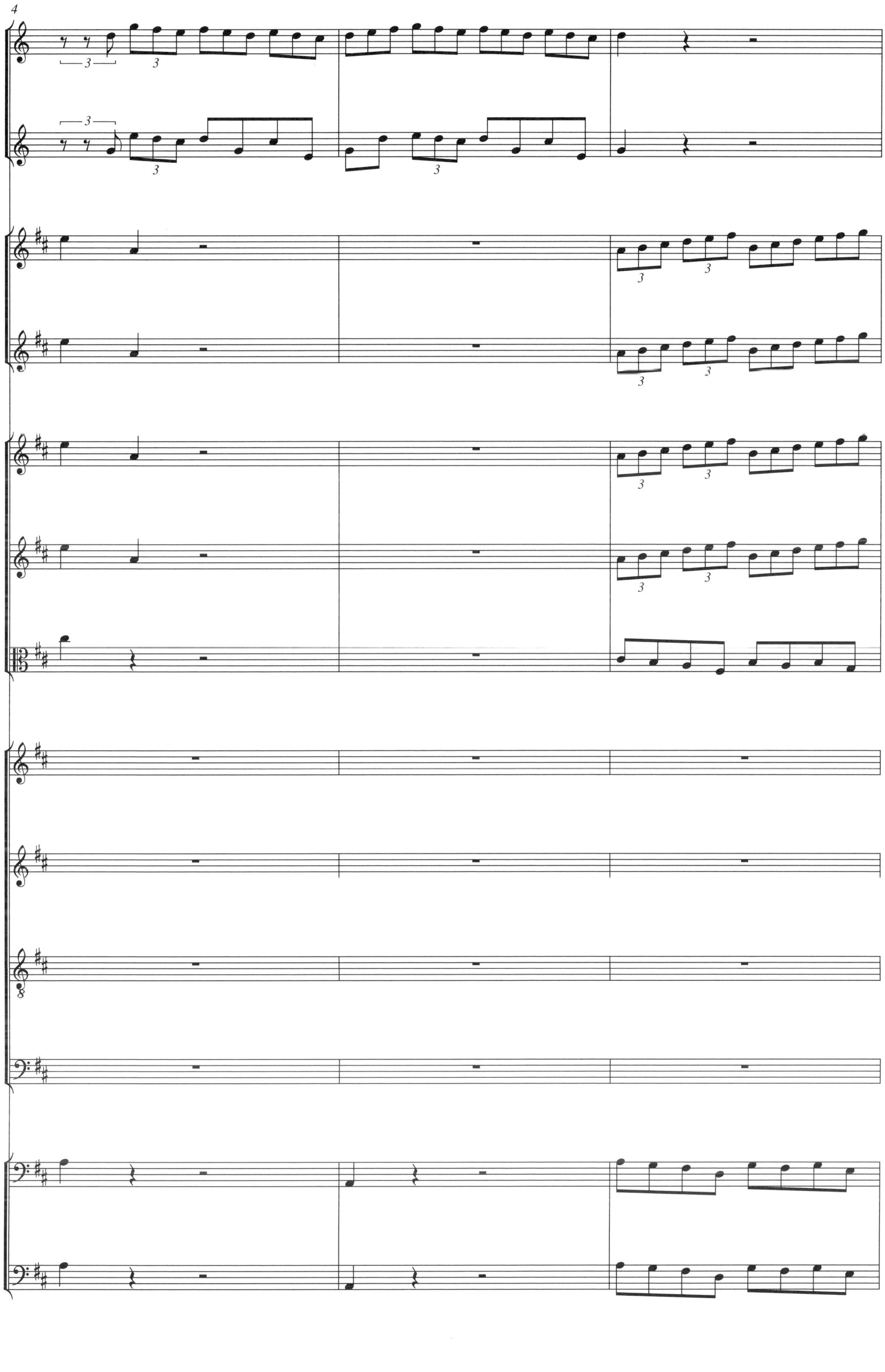

Lau- da, lau- da Je- ru- sa- lem Do- mi- num:
Lau- da, lau- da Je- ru- sa- lem Do- mi- num:
Lau- da, lau- da Je- ru- sa- lem Do- mi- num:
Lau- da, lau- da Je- ru- sa- lem Do- mi-

lau- da De- um tu- um Si- on. Quo- ni- am con- for-
lau- da De- um tu- um Si- on. Quo- ni- am con- for-
lau- da De- um tu- um, De- um tu- um Si- on. Quo- ni- am con- for-
-num: lau- da De- um tu- um, De- um tu- um Si- on. Quo- ni- am con- for-

-ta- vit se- ras por- ta- rum tu- a- rum: be- ne- di- xit fi- li- is tu- is in

-ta- vit se- ras por- ta- rum tu- a- rum: be- ne- di- xit fi- li- is tu- is in

-ta- vit se- ras por- ta- rum tu- a- rum: be- ne- di- xit fi- li- is tu- is in

-ta- vit se- ras por- ta- rum tu- a- rum: be- ne- di- xit fi- li- is tu- is in te.

22
tutti
Qui po- su- it fi- nes tu- os pa-
tutti
Qui po- su- it fi- nes tu- os pa-
[tutti]
pa- cem, pa-
[tutti]
pa- cem, pa-

-cem: et a- di- pe fru- men- ti sa- ti- at te. Qui e- mit- tit e-

30
-lo- qui- um su- um ter- rae: ve- lo- ci- ter cur- rit ser- mo e-
-lo- qui- um su- um ter- rae: ve- lo- ci- ter cur- rit ser- mo, ser- mo e-
-lo- qui- um su- um ter- rae: ve- lo- ci- ter cur- rit ser- mo, ser- mo e-
-lo- qui- um su- um ter- rae: ve- lo- ci- ter cur- rit ser- mo e- -

34
-jus. Qui dat ni- vem sic- ut la- nam: nu- be- cu- lam sic- ut
-jus. Qui dat ni- vem sic- ut la- - nam: nu- be- cu-lam sic- ut
-jus. Qui dat ni- vem sic- ut la- nam: nu- be- cu- lam sic- ut
-jus. Qui dat ni- vem sic- ut la- nam: nu- be- cu-lam sic- ut ci- ne- rem

38
ci- ne-rem spar- git.
ci- ne- rem spar- git.
ci- ne-rem spar- git.
spar- git.

Mit- tit cry- stal- lum su- am sic- ut buc-

-cel- - - las: an- te fa- ci- em fri- go- ris e- jus quis su- sti- ne- -bit, quis su- sti- ne- -

54
Hn. 1
Hn. 2
Ob. 1
Ob. 2
Vn. 1
Vn. 2
Va.
S
A
T
B
B.r.
B.c.
tutti
E- mit- tet ver- bum su- um, et
- bit? E- mit- tet ver- bum su- um, et li- que-
E- mit- tet ver- bum su- um, et li- que-
E- mit- tet ver- bum su- um, et li- que-

li- que- fa- ci- et e- a: fla- bit,
-fa- ci- et e- a:
-fa- ci- et e- a:
-fa- ci- et e- a:

61
Vn. 1
Vn. 2
S
p
p
fla- - - bit
65
spi- ri- tus e- jus, et flu- ent a- -
69
- - quae, et flu- ent a- quae, fla-
73
- - -
76
- bit spi- ri- tus e- jus, et flu- ent a- -

80
Hn. 1
Hn. 2
Ob. 1
Ob. 2
Vn. 1
Vn. 2
Va.
S
A
T
B
B.r.
B.c.
tutti
- quae. Qui an- nun- ti- at ver- bum su- um Ja- cob: ju-
Qui an- nun- ti- at ver- bum su- um Ja- cob:
Qui an- nun- ti- at ver- bum su- um Ja- cob:
Qui an- nun- ti- at ver- bum su- um Ja- cob:

-sti- ti- as et ju- di- ci- a su- a___ Is- ra-

ju- sti- ti- as et ju- di- ci- a su- a___ Is- ra-

ju- sti- ti- as et ju- di- ci- a su- a Is- ra-

ju- sti- ti- as et ju- di- ci- a su- a___ Is- ra-

-el. Non fecit taliter omni natio- ni: et judi- ci- a su- a non mani- fe-

91
Ob. 1
Ob. 2
Vn. 1
Vn. 2
Va.
S
-sta- vit c- is.
A
-sta- vit__ e- is.
T
tutti
-sta- vit e- is. Glo- ri- a
B
tutti
- vit__ e- is. Glo- ri- a
B.r.
B.c.
95
T
tr
Pa- tri, et Fi- li- o, et Spi- ri- tu- i San- cto.
B
[tr]
Pa- tri, et Fi- li- o, et Spi- ri- tu- i San- cto.
B.c.

102
Hn. 1
Hn. 2
Ob. 1
Ob. 2
Vn. 1
Vn. 2
Va.
S
Sic- ut e- rat in prin- ci- pi- o, et nunc, et nunc, et sem- per,
A
Sic- ut e- rat in prin- ci- pi- o, et nunc, et sem-
T
Sic- ut e- rat in prin- ci- pi- o, et nunc, et nunc, et sem- per,
B
Sic- ut e- rat in prin- ci- pi- o, et nunc, et sem- per,
B.r.
B.c.

105
sem- per, et in sae- cu- la sae- cu-
- per, sem- per, et in sae- -
nunc, et sem- per, et in sae- cu- la sae- cu- lo- rum,
sem- per, sem- per, et in sae- cu- la sae- cu- lo- rum,

109
-lo- rum. A- men, a- men, a- - men, a- men, a-
- cu- la sae- cu- lo- rum. A- men, a- men, a- men, a-
sae- cu- lo- - - rum. A- - men, a-
sae- cu- lo- rum. A- - men, a- - men, a-

113
-men, a- men, a- men, a- men.
-men, a- men, a- men, a- men.
-men, a- men, a- men, a- men.
-men, a- men, a- men, a- men.

Laudate pueri

4
Ob. 1
Ob. 2
Vn. 1
Vn. 2
Va.
S
A
B.r.
B.c.
à 2
Lau- da- te pu- e- ri Do- mi- num: lau- da- te no- men
[à 2]
Lau- da- te pu- e- ri Do- mi- num: lau- da- te
7
Do- mi- ni. Sit no- men Do- mi- ni be- ne- di- ctum, ex hoc nunc, et u- sque in sae- cu-
no- men Do- mi- ni. Sit no- men Do- mi- ni be- ne- di- ctum, ex hoc nunc, et u- sque in sae- cu-
10
p
-lum.
-lum.
solo
B
A so- lis or- tu u- sque ad oc- ca- - sum, lau-

110

16
su-per cae- los, su- per cae- los glo- - ri- a e- jus,
su-per cae- los, et su- per cae- los, su- per cae- los glo- ri- a e- jus,
- los, su- per cae- - los glo- ri- a, glo- ri- a, glo- ri- a e- jus,
- los, et su- per cae- - los, su- per cae- los glo- ri- a e- jus,

19
su- per cae- los glo- ri- a, glo- ri- a,glo- ri- a e- jus.
su- per cae- los glo- ri- a, glo- ri- a e- jus.
su- per cae- los glo- ri- a e- jus, glo- ri- a e- jus.
su- per cae- los glo- ri- a, glo- ri- a e- jus.
22
Ob. 1
Ob. 2
Vn. 1
Vn. 2
Va.
B.r.
B.c.

25
Ob. 1
Ob. 2
Vn. 1
Vn. 2
Va.
T
[solo]
Quis sic- ut Do- mi-nus De- us no- ster, qui in al- tis ha- bi-
B.r.
B.c.
28
-tat, et hu- mi- li- a re- spi- cit in cae- lo et in ter- ra?
[7]
7 6
6 7 6

Su- sci-tans a ter- ra in- o- pem, et de ster- co- re e- ri-gens pau- pe-rem: Ut col- lo- cet

Su- sci-tans a ter- ra in- o- pem, et de ster- co- re e- ri-gens pau- pe-rem: Ut

Su- sci-tans a ter- ra in- o- pem, et de ster- co- re e- ri-gens pau- pe-rem: Ut

Su- sci-tans a ter- ra in- o- pem, et de ster- co- re e- ri-gens pau- pe-rem: Ut e- um cum prin- ci- pi-bus, cum prin- ci- pi- bus po- pu- li su- i. Qui ha- bi- ta- re fa- cit

col- lo-cet e- um cum prin- ci- pi- bus, cum prin- ci- pi- bus po- pu- li su- i. Qui ha- bi- ta- re fa- cit

col- lo-cet e- um cum prin- ci- pi- bus, cum prin- ci- pi- bus po- pu- li su- i. Qui ha- bi- ta- re fa- cit

col- lo-cet e- um cum prin- ci- pi- bus, cum prin- ci- pi- bus po- pu- li su- i. Qui ha- bi- ta- re fa- cit

38
ste- ri-lem in do- mo, ma-trem fi- li- o- rum lae-tan-tem, lae-
ste- ri-lem in do- mo, ma-trem fi- li- o- rum, fi- li- o- rum lae-tan-tem, lae-
ste- ri-lem in do- mo, ma-trem fi- li- o- rum, fi- li- o- rum lae- tan-tem, lae-
ste- ri-lem in do- mo, ma-trem fi- li- o- - rum lae-tan- tem, [lae-
[♯] [6 4] [♯]

41
-tan- tem, lae- tan- - tem, lae tan- tem, lae- tan- tem.
-tan- tem, lae- tan- tem, lae- tan- tem, lae-tan- tem.
-tan- tem, lae- tan- - tem, lae- tan- tem.
-tan-tem,] lae- tan- - tem, lae- tan- tem.

44
Ob. 1
Ob. 2
Vn. 1
Vn. 2
Va.
B
B.r.
B.c.
p
solo
Glo- ri-a Pa- tri,
47
Vn. 1
Vn. 2
Va.
S
A
B
B.c.
[𝄐]
à 2
[à 2]
Sic- ut e- rat in prin-
glo- ri-a Fi- li- o, glo- ri-a et Spi- ri- tu- i San- cto.

119

57
- per, et in sae- cu- la, in sae-cu-la sae- cu- lo-rum, a-
sem- per, et in sae- cu- la, in sae-cu-la sae- cu- lo-rum, a- men, a-
sem- per, et in sae- cu- la, in sae- cu-la sae- cu- lo- - rum, sae- cu-
sem- per, et _ in] sae- cu- la, in sae- cu-la sae- cu- lo-rum, a- - men, [a-

60
- men, a- men, a- men, a- men, a- men, a- men,
- men, a- men, a- men, a- men, a- men, a- men,
-lo- rum, a- men, a- men, a- men, a- men, a- men, a-
- men, a- men,] a- men, a- men, a- men, a- men, a-

62
a- men, a- - men, a- men, a- men.
a- - men, a- men, a- men.
- men, a- men, a- - men, a- men.
- - men, a- men, a- men.

Nisi Dominus

-di- fi- ca- ve-rit do- mum, in va-num la- bo- ra- ve- - runt, la- bo- ra- ve- runt, in va- num la- bo- ra- ve- runt,

in va- num, in va- num la- bo- ra- ve- runt qui ae- di- fi-cant e- am.

Ni- si Do- mi-nus cu- sto- di- e- rit ci- vi- ta- tem, fru- stra vi- gi- lat, fru- stra

fru- stra vi- gi- lat,

vi- gi- lat qui cu- sto- dit e- am.

Va- num est

vo- bis an- te lu- cem sur- ge- re: sur- gi- te post- quam se- de- ri- tis, qui man- du- ca- tis pa- nem do-

-lo- ris.

Cum de- de-rit di- le-ctis su- is som-

-num: ec- ce hae- re- di-tas Do- mi- ni, fi- li- i: mer- ces, fru-ctus ven-

35
-tris.
Sic- ut sa- git- tae in ma- nu po-ten- tis: i- ta fi- li- i ex- cus- so-
38
Be- a- tus vir, be-a- tus vir qui im-ple- vit
- rum.

de- si- de- ri-um su- um ex i- psis: non con-fun-de- tur cum lo- que- tur i- ni-mi-cis

su- is,

non con- fun- de- tur cum lo- que- tur i- ni- mi- cis su- is in por- ta.

Glo- ri- a Pa- tri, et Fi- li- o, et Spi- ri- tu- i San- cto. Sic- ut e- rat

56
in prin- ci- pi- o, et nunc, et sem- per, sem- per, et in
et nunc, et sem- per,
59
sae- cu- la sae- cu- lo- rum. A- men, a- men, a-
A-

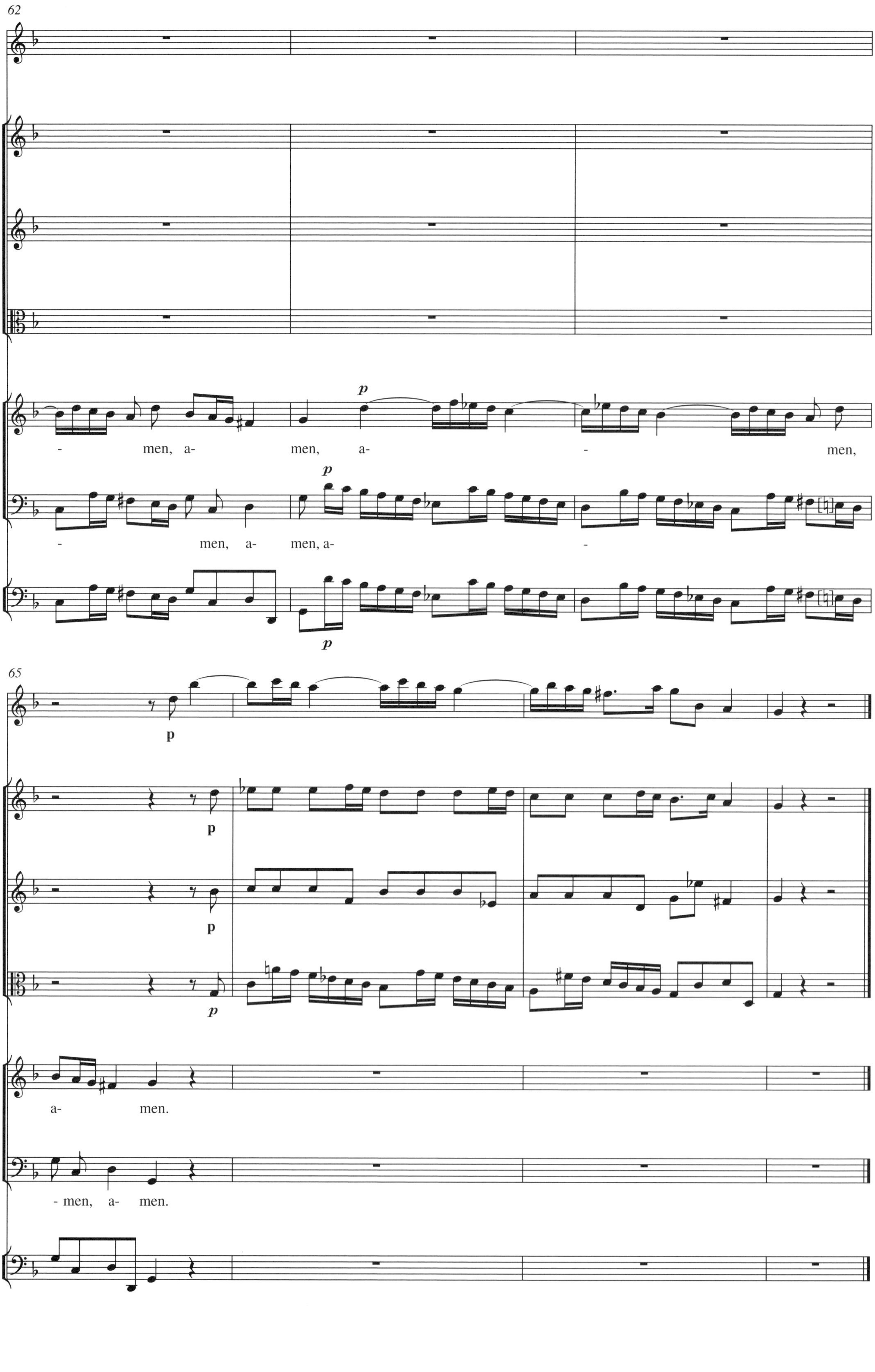
62
p
men, a-
men, a-
men,
men, a-
men, a-
65
a-
men.
men, a-
men.

Magnificats

Magnificat in G

1. Magnificat

8
Adagio
[a tempo]
f
Adagio
[a tempo]
Ma- gni- fi- cat a- ni- ma me- a
Ma- gni- fi- cat a- ni- ma me- a
Ma- gni- fi- cat a- ni- ma me- a
-gni- fi- cat, ma- - gni- - fi-
13
Do- mi- num, ma- - gni-
Do- mi- num, ma- gni- fi- cat a- ni- ma me- a
Do- mi- num, ma- gni- fi- cat a- ni- ma me- a
-cat, ma- gni- fi- cat a- ni- ma me- a

16
- fi- cat. Et ex- sul- ta- -
Do- mi- num. Et ex- sul- ta- vit, et ex- sul-ta- - vit
Do- mi- num. Et ex- sul- ta- -
Do- mi- num. Et ex- sul- ta- vit, et ex- sul-ta- -
20
-vit, et ex- sul- ta- vit, ex- sul- ta- vit spi- ri- tus me- us, et ex- sul-
spi- ri- tus me- us, et ex- sul-
- vit, ex- sul- ta- vit, ex- sul- ta- vit spi- ri- tus me- us, ex- sul- ta-
- vit spi- ri- tus me- us, et ex- sul- ta-

23
-ta- - vit, et ex- sul- ta- vit, ex- sul- ta- vit
-ta- - vit, et ex- sul- ta- vit spi- ri- tus
- - - vit, ex- sul- ta- vit, ex- sul- ta-
- - - vit, et ex- sul- ta- vit, ex- sul- ta- vit
6

27
spi- ri- tus me- us in De- o sa- lu- ta- ri me- o, in De- o
me- us in De- o sa- lu- ta- ri me- o, in De- o___ sa- lu-
- vit spi- ri- tus me- us in De- o, in
spi- ri- tus me- us in De- o sa- lu- ta- ri me- o, in De- o

139

2. Quia respexit

141

qui po- tens est: et san- ctum no- men e- jus. Et mi- se- ri-
-cor- di- a e- jus a pro- ge- ni- e in pro- ge- ni- es ti- men- ti- bus
e- um, et mi- se- ri- cor- di- a e- jus a pro- ge- ni- e in pro-

-ge- ni- es ti- men- - - ti- bus e- um.

3. Fecit potentiam

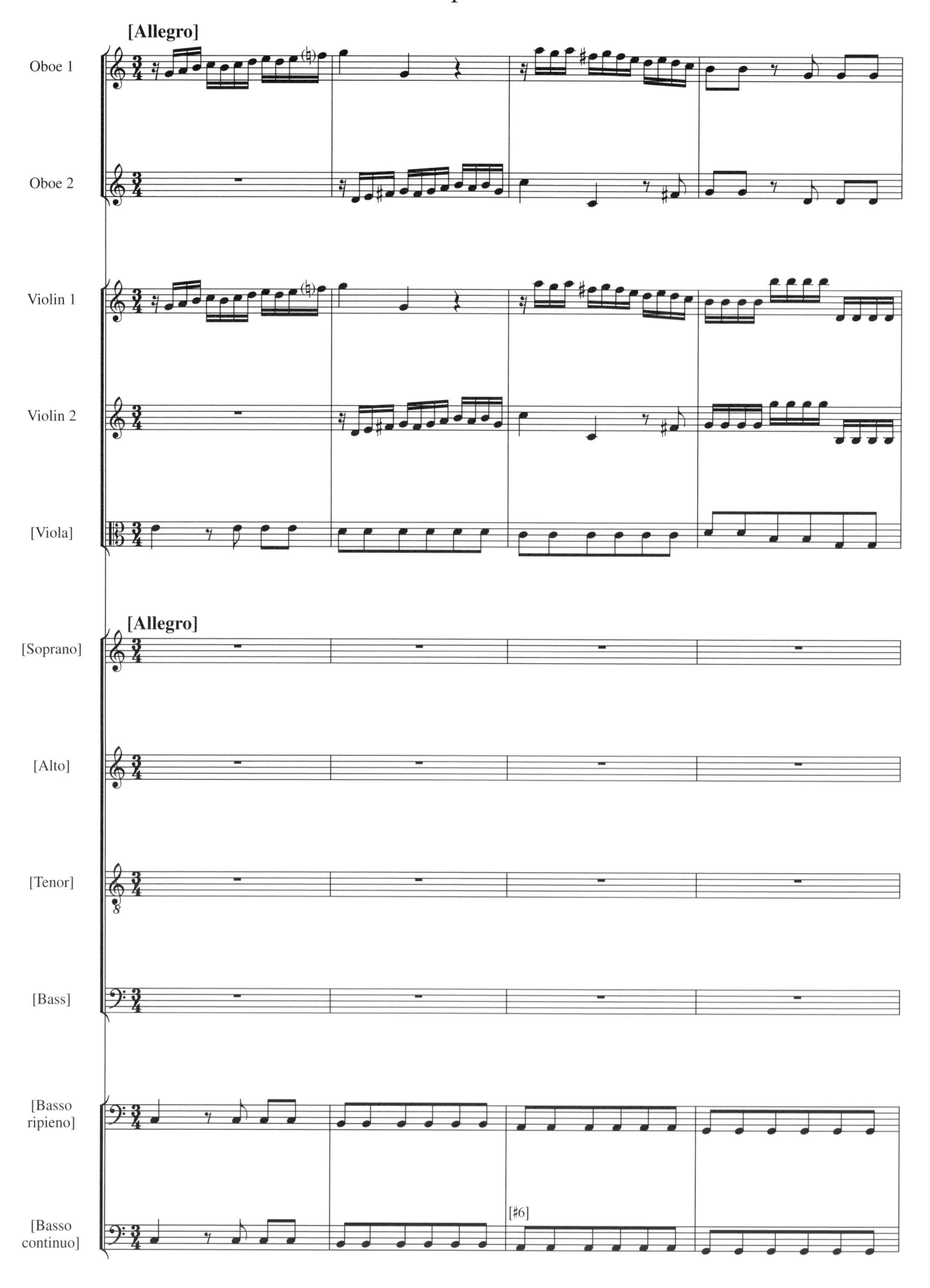

5
Fe- cit po- ten- ti- am, po- ten-
Fe- cit po- ten- ti- am, po- ten-
Fe- cit po- ten- ti- am, po- ten-
Fe- cit po- ten- ti- am, po- ten-

9
- ti-am, fe- cit po- ten- ti- am, po- ten- - ti-am in bra-chi-o
- ti-am, fe- cit po- ten- ti- am, po- ten- - ti-am in bra-chi-o
- ti-am, fe- cit po- ten- ti- am, po- ten- - ti-am in bra-chi-o
- ti-am, fe- cit po- ten- ti- am, po- ten- - ti-am in bra-chi-o

su- o, in bra- chi- o su- o: di- sper- sit, di- sper- sit,

su- o, in bra- chi- o su- o: di- sper- sit, di- sper-

su- o, in bra- chi- o su- o: di- sper- sit,

su- o, in bra- chi- o su- o: di- sper- sit su-

17
di- sper- sit, di- sper- - - sit,
- sit, di- sper- - sit, di- sper-
di- sper- - sit, di- sper- - sit, di-
-per- bos, su- per-

21
di- sper- - - sit su- per- bos, di- sper-
- sit, di- sper- - - sit, di- sper-
-sper- sit su- per- bos, di- sper-
-bos, su- per- bos, di- sper-
[♯]

- sit super - bos, su- per- bos men- te cor- dis su- i.

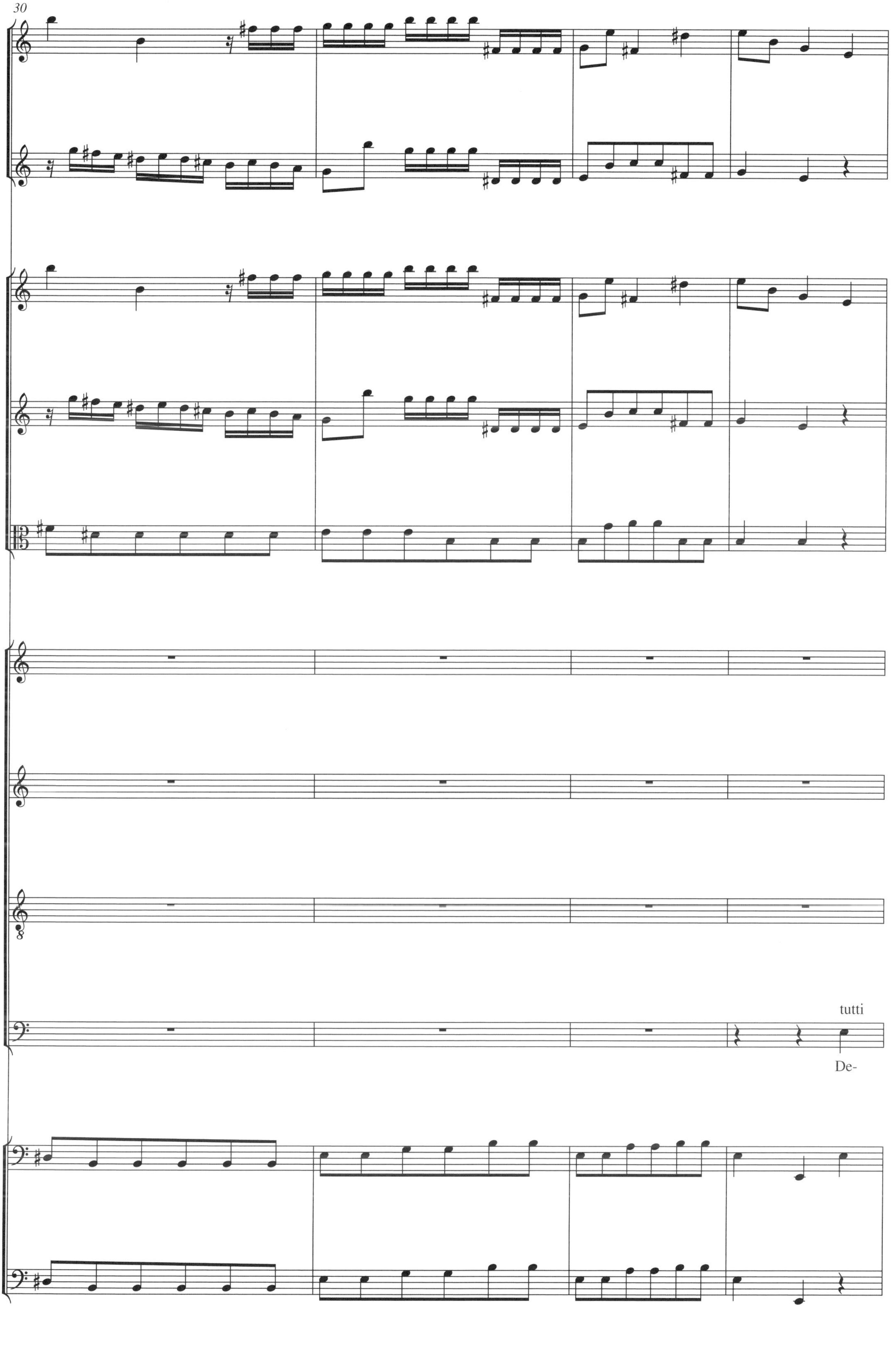
30
tutti
De-

34
De- po- su- it po- ten-
De- po- su- it po- ten-
De- po- su- it po- ten-
-po- - - su- it, de- po- su- it po- ten-

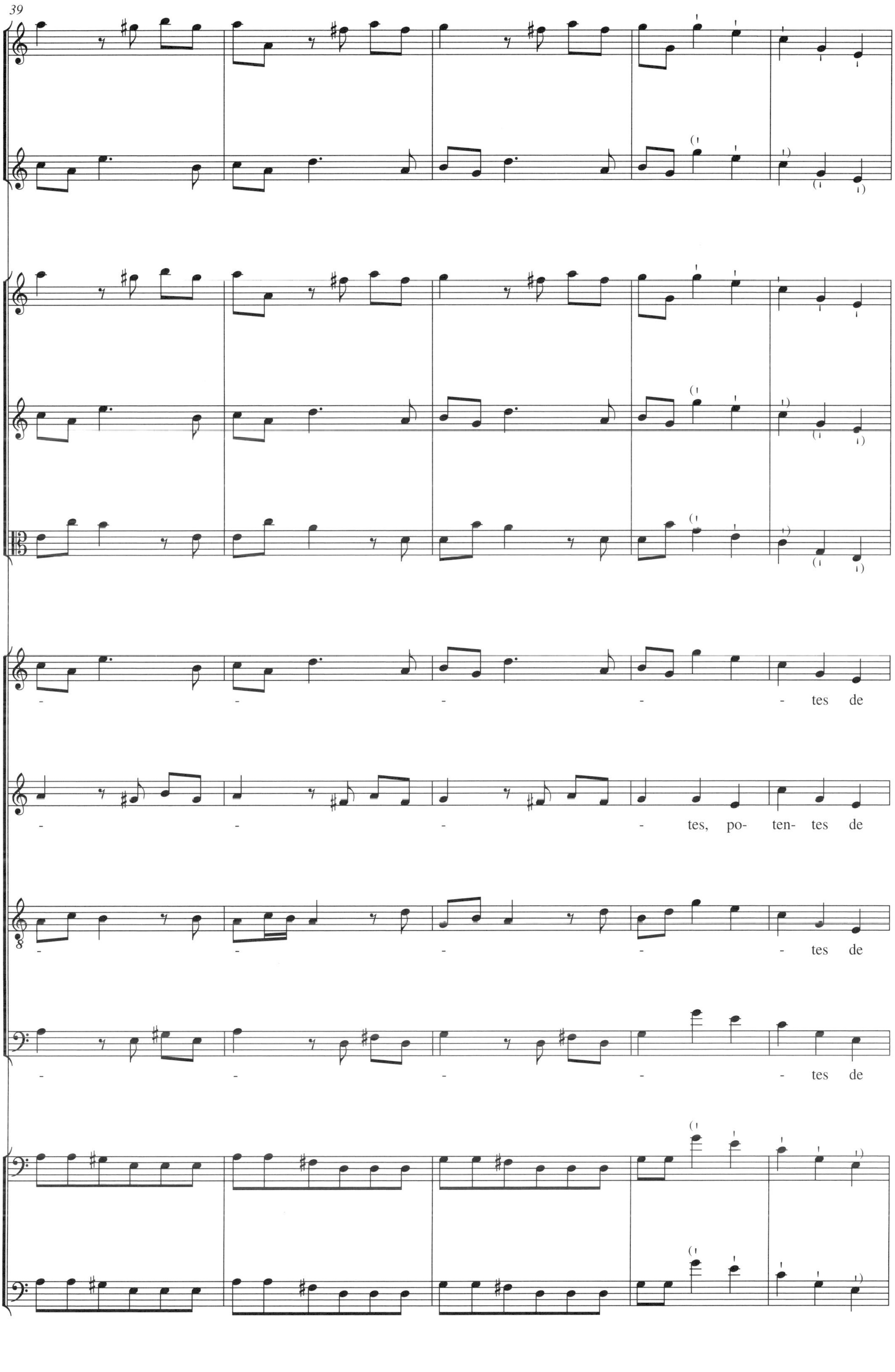
39
tes de
tes, po- ten- tes de
tes de
tes de

44
Adagio
Adagio
se- de, et ex- al- ta- - vit hu- mi- les, hu- mi-
se- de, et ex- al- ta- vit hu- mi- les, hu- mi-
se- de, et ex- al- ta- vit hu- mi- les, hu- mi-
se- de, et ex- al- ta- vit hu- mi- les, hu- mi-

-les. E- su- ri- en- tes im- ple- vit bo- nis, e- su ri-

53
-en- tes im- ple- vit bo- nis, im- ple- -
-en- tes im- ple- vit bo- nis, im- ple- - -
-en- tes im- ple- vit bo- nis, im- ple- -
-en- tes im- ple- vit bo- nis, im- ple- - -

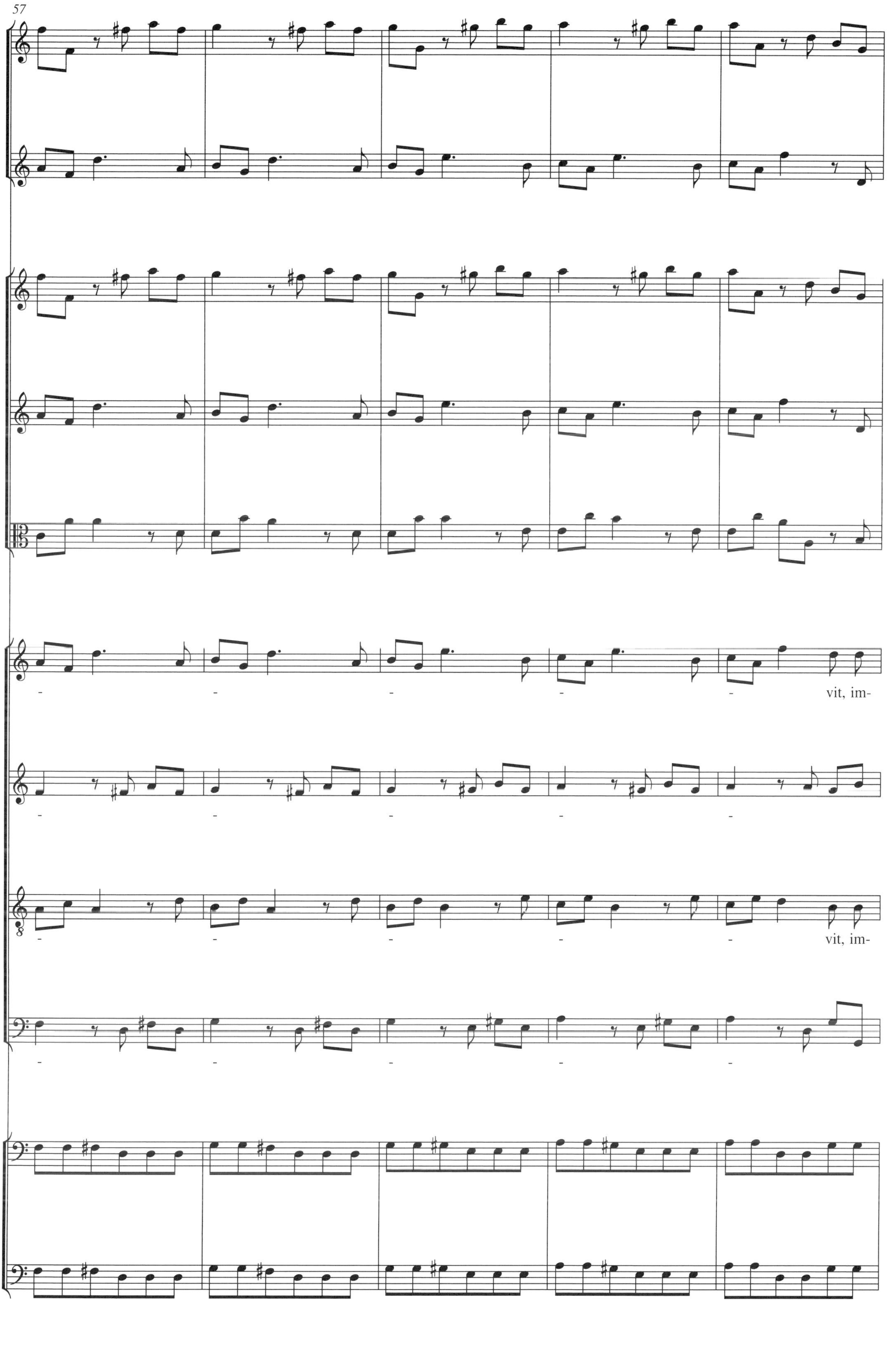
57
vit, im-
vit, im-

-plevit bonis, implevit bonis: et divites dimisit inanes.

4. Suscepit Israel

14
sus- ce- pit Is- ra- el pu- e- rum su- um, re-
20
- cor-da- - tus mi- se- ri- cor- - - - di- ae

su- ae, sus- ce- pit Is- ra- el pu- e- rum su- um, re- cor- da- tus mi-

41
-se- ri- cor- di- ae su- ae. Sic- ut lo- cu- tus est ad
6 ♭7 6
7 6
48
pa- tres no- stros, A- bra-ham et se- mi- ni e- jus in sae- - cu- la,
7
5

in sae- - - cu- la.

5. Gloria

6. Sicut erat in principio

Sic- ut e- rat in prin- ci- pi- o, et nunc, et nunc, et__ sem-

*For this movement, the basso ripieno comprises violoncello, theorbo, bassoon, and double bass.

4
- - per, et in sae- cu- la sae- cu- lo- - rum, a-
Sic- ut e- rat in prin- ci- pi- o, et nunc, et nunc, et sem- - per, sem- per, sem-

167

12
- - men, a- -
a- - men, a- - men,
- - per, et in sae- cu- la sae- cu- lo- rum,
in prin- ci- pi- o, et nunc, et sem- - per, sem- per, et in

15
- men, et in sae- cu- la sae- cu- lo- rum, a- - men, a- men, a- men,
a- - men, sic- ut e- rat
a- men, et in sae- cu- la sae- cu- lo- rum, a- - men, a- men, a- men, a-
sae- cu- la sae- cu- lo- rum, a- men, a-

in prin-ci- pi- o, et nunc, et sem- - per, et in sae- cu- la - men, sic- ut e- rat in prin- ci- pi- o, et - men, a- - men, a- men,

[tasto solo]

sae- cu- lo- rum, a- - - nunc, et sem- - per, sem- per, et in sae- - cu- la___ sae- cu-

sic- ut e- rat in prin- ci- pi- o, et

sic- ut e- rat in prin-ci- pi- o, et nunc, et sem-
- men, a- - men, a- - men, a- men,
-lo- - rum, a- - men, a-
nunc, et sem- - per, sem- per,

[♮6]

- per, sem- per, sem- per, et___ in sae- cu- la sae- cu- lo- rum, a-
a- men, a- men, et___ in sae- cu- la sae- cu- lo- rum, a-
- men, a- - - men, a- men,
sic- ut e- rat in prin-ci- pi- o, et nunc, et sem- per, et in___

- men, a- men, a- men, et in sae- cu- la sae- cu- lo -
- men, a- men, a- men, et in sae- cu- la sae- cu- lo -
a- men, a- men, a- men, sic- ut e- rat in prin- ci- pi- o, et
sae- cu- la sae- cu- lo - rum, a- men, sic- ut e- rat in prin- ci- pi- o, et

175

Magnificat in B-flat

1. Magnificat

177

7
Ma- gni- fi- cat a- ni- ma
Ma- gni- fi- cat a- ni- ma
Ma- gni- fi- cat a- ni- ma
Ma- gni- fi- cat a- ni- ma
[♭7]

10
me- a Do- mi- num, ma- gni- fi- cat a- - ni- ma me- a Do-
me- a Do- mi- num, ma- gni- fi- cat a- ni- ma me- a
me- a Do- mi- num, ma- gni- fi- cat a- ni- ma me- a
me- a Do- mi- num, ma- gni- fi- cat a- ni- ma me- a
[6 4]
[5 3]

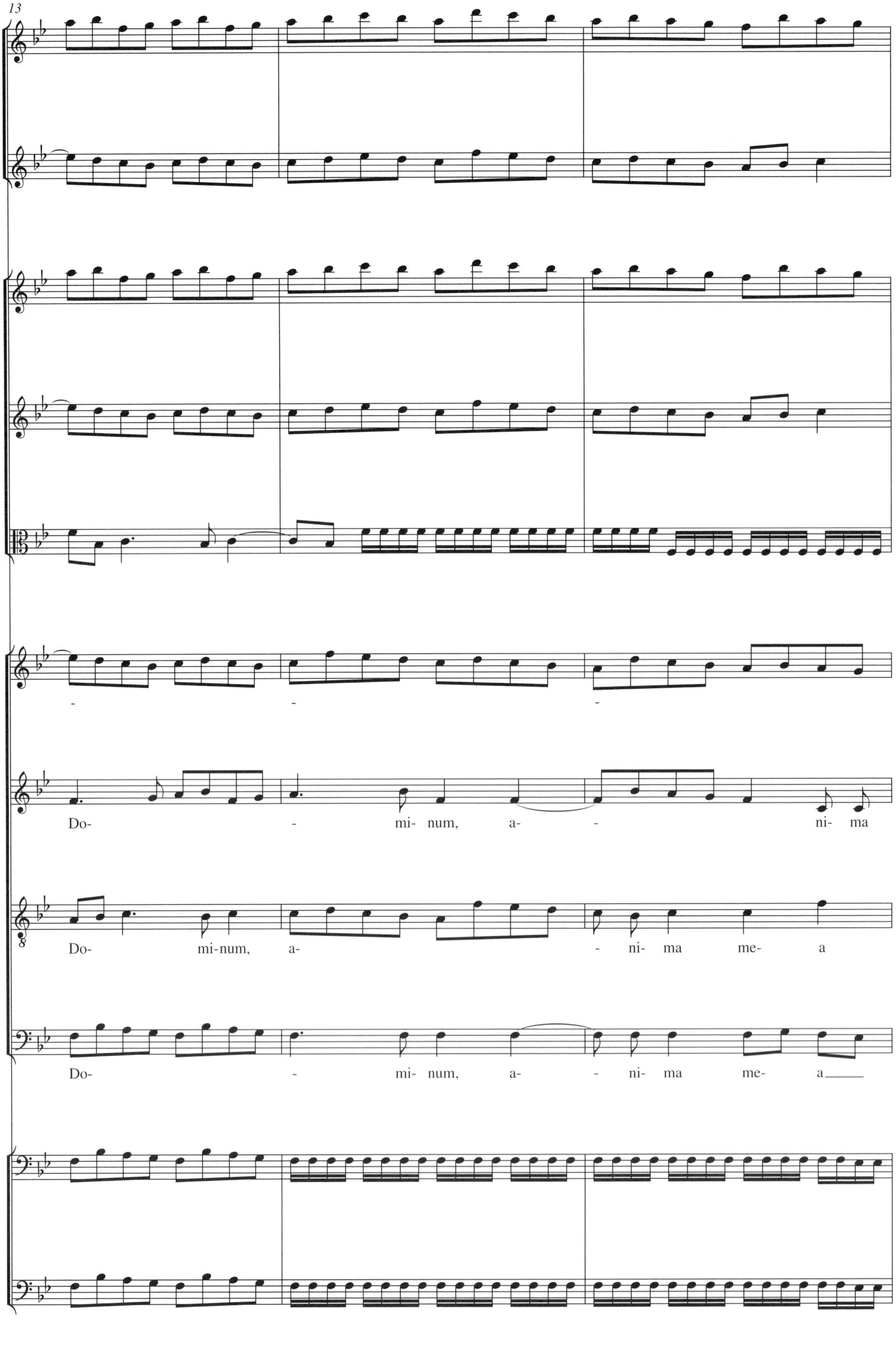
13
- - -
Do- - mi- num, a- - ni- ma
Do- mi-num, a- - ni- ma me- a
Do- - mi- num, a- - ni- ma me- a

181

19
Ob. 1
Ob. 2
Vn. 1
Vn. 2
Va.
f
solo
Et ex- sul- ta- - vit,
S
tutti
Et ex- sul-
A
[tutti]
Et ex- sul-
T
[tutti]
Et ex- sul-
B
[tutti]
Et ex- sul-
B.r.
B.c.

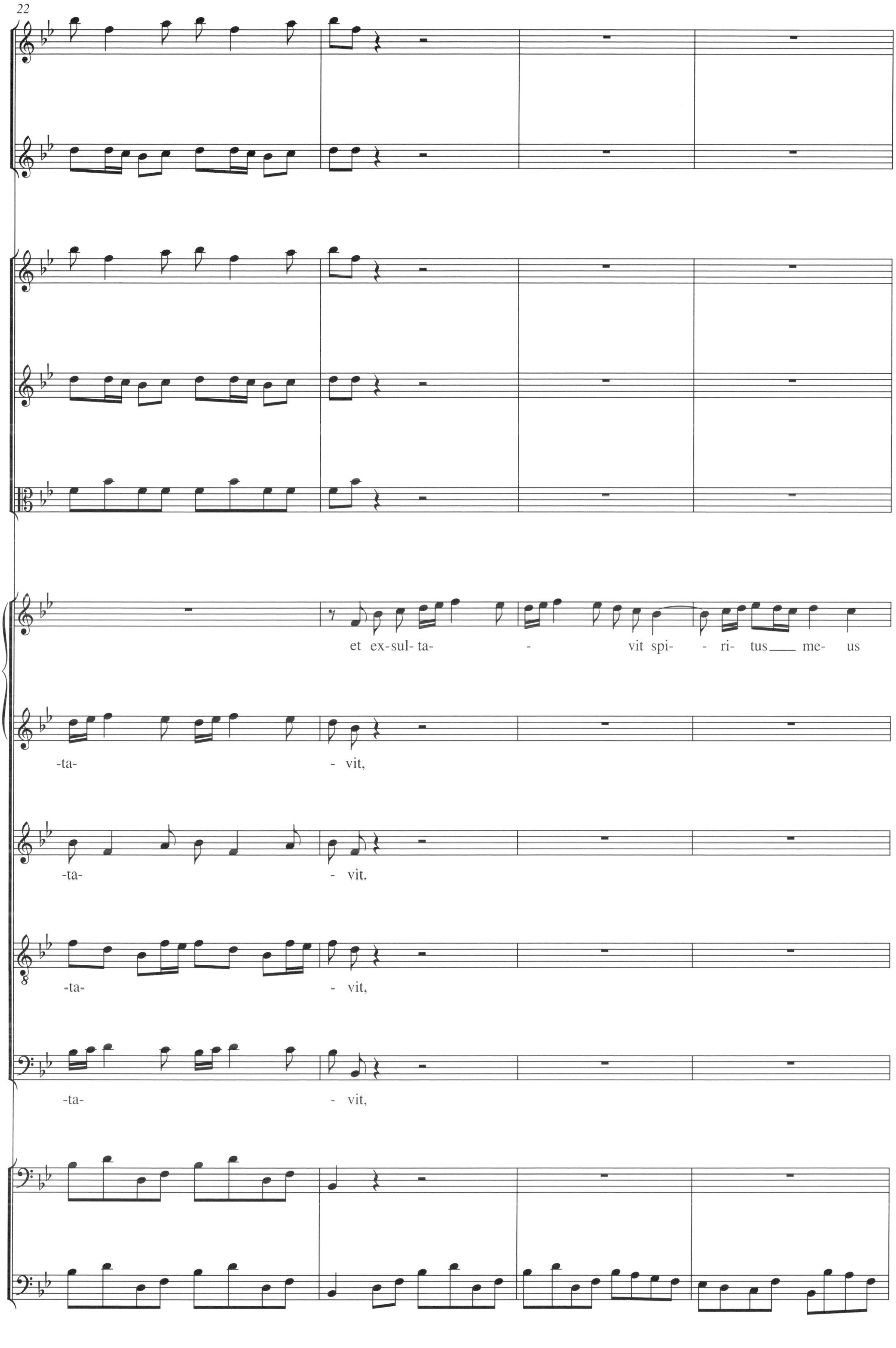
22
et ex-sul-ta- - vit spi- - ri- tus me- us
-ta- - vit,
-ta- - vit,
-ta- - vit,
-ta- - vit,

26
[tutti]
in De- o sa- lu- ta- - ri me- o, in De- o
tutti
in De- o
[tutti]
in De- o
[tutti]
in De- o
[tutti]
in De- o

30
Ob. 1
Ob. 2
Vn. 1
Vn. 2
Va.
S
sa- lu- ta- - - ri me- o, in De- o sa- lu-
A
sa- lu- ta- - - ri me- o, in De- o sa- lu- ta-
T
sa- lu- ta- ri, sa- lu- ta- - ri me- o, in De- o sa- lu- ta- ri,
B
sa- lu- ta- ri, sa- lu- ta- - ri me- o, in De- o sa- lu- ta- ri,
B.r.
B.c.

34
pp
pp
pp
-ta- ri me- o.
- ri me- o.
sa- lu- ta- ri me- o.
sa- lu- ta- ri me- o.
pp
6 4 2
7 4 2
6 4 2
7 4 2
pp

2. Quia respexit

11
-spe- xit hu- mi- li- ta- - tem an- cil- - lae su- ae: ec- ce e- nim ex
[♭] [♭] [7]
17
hoc be- a- - - - tam me di- cent
[6 4] [♮]

22
om-nes ge- ne- ra- - ti- o- nes.
[6 4]
28
Qui- a fe- cit mi- hi ma- gna qui po- tens est, qui po-

33
- - - - tens, qui po- tens est:
[♭]
38
et san- ctum no- men, et san- ctum no- men e- jus.
[♭7]
[♭]

Et mi- se- ri- cor- di- a e- jus, et mi- se- ri- cor- di- a

senza organo

56
e- jus a pro- ge- ni- e in pro- ge- ni- es ti- men- - - ti- bus
[♭7] [♭] [♭7] [6]
62
e- um, ti- men- - -
[6 4]
organo

- ti- bus e- um.

3. Fecit potentiam

*For this movement, bassoons are omitted from the basso ripieno group.

Vn. 1
Vn. 2
Va.
Bn. solo 1
Bn. solo 2
B.r.
B.c.
B solo 1
Fe-cit po-ten- ti-am, po- ten-
B solo 2
Fe- cit po- ten- ti-am,

8
Ob. 1
Ob. 2
Vn. 1
Vn. 2
Va.
S
A
T
B
B solo 1
- ti-am in bra- chi- o, in bra- chi-o su-
B solo 2
po- ten- - ti-am in bra- - chi-o, in bra-chi-o su-
Bn. solo 1
Bn. solo 2
B.r.
B.c.

dispersit superbos mente cordis sui, dispersit, di-

-sersit, di- sper- sit su- per- bos men- te cor- dis, su- per- bos men- te cor- dis su-

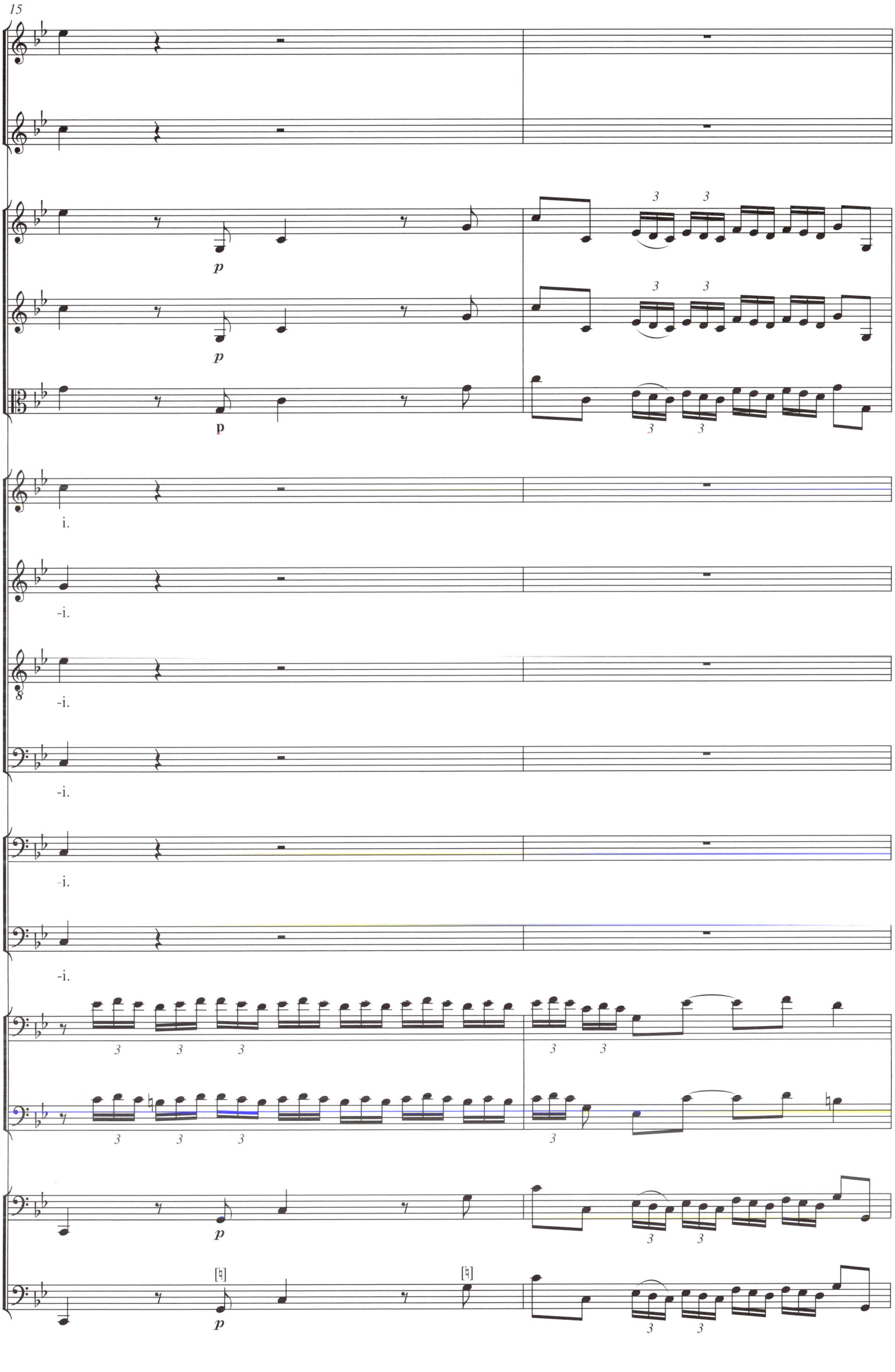
15
p
p
p
i.
-i.
-i.
-i.
-i.
-i.
p
[♮]
[♮]
p

17
De- po- su- it po- ten- tes, po- ten- tes de se- de,
De- po- su- it po- ten- tes, po- ten- tes de

20
f
De- po- su- it po-
De- po- su- it po-
De- po- su- it po-
De- po- su- it po-
po- ten- tes de se- de, de- po- su- it po-
se- de, po- ten- tes de se- de, de- po- su- it po-
[♭]

22
-ten- tes, po- ten- tes, de- po- su- it po-ten- tes de se- de, et
-ten- tes, po- ten- tes, de- po- su- it po-ten- tes de se- de, et
-ten- tes, po- ten- tes, de- po- su- it po-ten- tes de se- de, et
-ten- tes, po- ten- tes, de- po- su- it po-ten- tes de se- de, et
-ten- [tes, po]- ten- - tes, po- ten-
-ten- tes, po- ten- - tes de se- de, po- ten-
[♮]

24
ex- al- ta- vit hu- mi- les.
ex- al- ta- vit hu- mi- les.
ex- al- ta- vit hu- mi- les.
ex- al- ta- vit hu- mi- les.
- tes, et ex- al- ta- vit hu- mi- lcs.
- tes, et ex- al- ta- vit hu- mi- les.

E- su- ri- en- tes im-ple-vit bo-nis, im-ple- vit, im-ple- vit

E- su- ri- en- tes im-ple-vit bo-nis, im- ple-vit,

29
f
im- ple- vit bo- nis, im- ple- vit
im- ple- vit bo- nis, im- ple- vit
im- ple- vit bo- nis, im- ple- vit
im- ple- vit bo- nis, im- ple- vit
bo- nis, im- ple- vit bo- nis: et di- vi- tes di- mi- sit i-
im- ple- vit bo- nis, im- ple- vit: et di- vi- tes di- mi- sit

31
bo- nis: et di- vi- tes di- mi- sit i- na- nes, et di- vi- tes di- mi- sit i-
bo- nis: et di- vi- tes di- mi- sit i- na- nes, et di- vi- tes di- mi- sit i-
bo- nis: et di- vi- tes di- mi- sit i- na- nes, et di- vi- tes di- mi- sit i-
bo- nis: et di- vi- tes di- mi- sit i- na- nes, et di- vi- tes di- mi- sit i-
-na- nes, i- na- nes, i-
i- na- nes, i- na- nes, i-
[♮]

33
-na- nes, i- na-
-na- nes, i- na-
-na- nes, i- na-
-na- nes, i- na-
-na- ncs, i- na- nes, i
-na- nes, i- na- nes, i-

35
-nes, et di- vi- tes di- mi- sit i- na- nes, i- na- nes, i- na- nes.
-nes, et di- vi- tes di- mi- sit i- na- nes, i- na- nes, i- na- nes.
-nes, et di- vi- tes di- mi- sit i- na- nes, i- na- nes, i- na- nes.
-nes, et di- vi- tes di- mi- sit i- na- nes, i- na- nes, i- na- nes.
-na- nes, et di- vi- tes di- mi- sit i- na- nes, i- na- nes, i- na- nes.
-na- nes, et di- vi- tes di- mi- sit i- na- nes, i- na- nes, i- na- nes.

4. Suscepit Israel

12
re- cor- da- - tus mi- se- ri- cor- - - di-ae su-
18
-ae, sus- ce- pit Is- ra- el pu- e- rum su- um, re- cor- da- tus mi-

24
-se- ri- cor- - - di- ae su- ae. Sic- ut lo- cu- tus_ est ad
30
pa- tres no- stros, A- bra- ham et se- mi- ni e- jus in sae- - cu-
[♭]

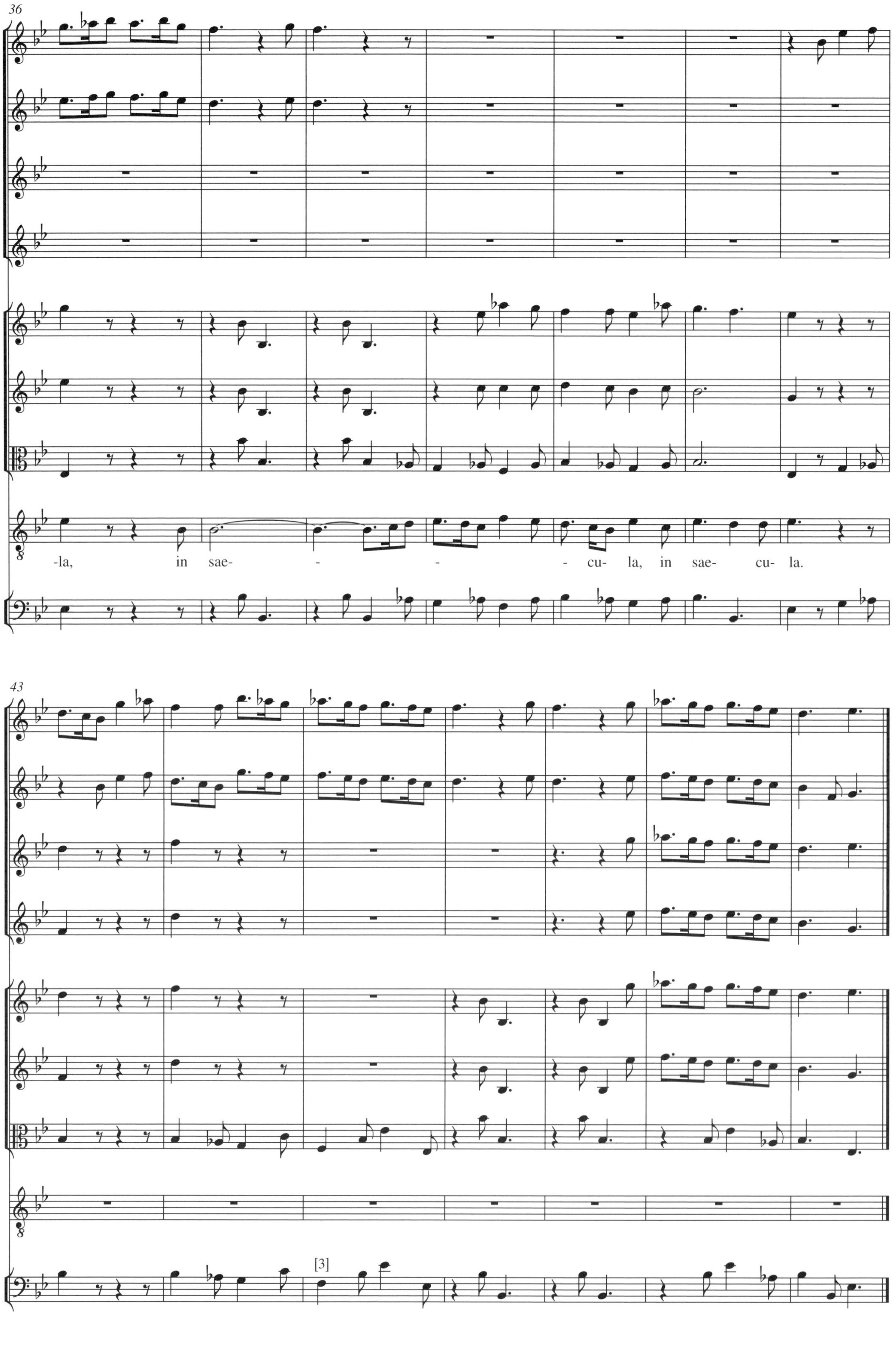
36
-la, in sae- - - -cu- la, in sae- cu- la.
43
[3]

5. Gloria

*For this movement, the basso ripieno comprises violoncello, theorbo, bassoon, and double bass.

Sic- ut— e- rat in— prin- ci- pi- o, et— nunc, et nunc, et sem— per, et— in— sae- cu- la—

Sic- ut— e- rat

[tasto solo]

9
sae-cu- lo-rum, a- men, sae- - cu- lo- rum, a- - men, sae- cu- lo-rum, a- men, a-
in prin- ci- pi- o, et nunc, et nunc, et sem- per, sem- per, et in sae-cu- la sae-cu- lo-
Sic- ut e- rat in prin- ci- pi- o, et
[5]

216

sic- ut e- rat in prin-ci- pi- o, et nunc, et sem-per, et in et in sae- cu- la sae- cu- lo- rum,_ a-

sic- ut e- rat in prin-ci- pi- o, et nunc, et sem-per, et in sae- cu- la sae-cu- lo- rum, a-

sem-per, sic- ut e- rat in prin-ci- pi-

21
sae- cu- la sae- cu- lo-rum, a- - -
- men, a- - men, a- - men,
-men, a- - men, a- - - men, et in
-o, et nunc, et sem-per, et in sae- cu- la sae- cu- lo- rum, a- - men, et in

219

in— prin- ci- pi- o, et— nunc, et nunc, et sem- per, et in— sae- - cu- la sae- cu-
sae- cu- lo- rum, a- men, a- - men, sae- cu-

sic- ut— e- rat

-lo- rum, a- men, a- men, a- - - -

-lo- rum, a- - men, a- - men, a-

in prin- ci- pi- o, et nunc, et nunc, et sem- per, et in sae- cu- la

sic- ut e- rat in prin- ci- pi- o, et

37
- men, et in sae- cu- la sae- cu- lo-
-men, a- men, sic- ut e- rat in prin-ci- pi- o, et nunc, et nunc, et sem-per, et in sae-cu- la sae-cu-
sae- cu- lo- rum, sic- ut e- rat in prin-ci- pi- o, et nunc, et nunc, et sem- per, et in sae-cu-
nunc, et nunc, et sem- per, sic- ut e- rat in prin-ci- pi- o, et nunc, et nunc, et sem-per, et in

-rum, a- men, saeculorum, a- men, a- men.

-lorum, a- men, sae- cu- lo-rum, a- men, sae- cu- lo-rum, a- men, a- men.

-la sae-cu-lo-rum, a- men, a- men, sae- cu- lo- rum, a- men, a- men.

sae- cu- la sae- cu- lo- rum, a- men, sae- cu- lo- rum, a- men, a- men.

Hymns

Ave maris stella

*For this setting, the basso ripieno comprises violoncello, theorbo, bassoon, and double bass.

16
al- ma, At- que sem- per, sem- per Vir-
At- que sem- per Vir- go, sem- per Vir- go,
sem- per, sem- - per Vir- - go,
Ma- - ter al- ma, At- que sem- per

23
-go, Fe- - lix cae- li por- - ta.
Fe- - lix cae- - - - li
Fe- lix, fe- - lix cae- li, cae- - li
Vir- go, Fe- - - lix cae- li

30
Su- mens il- lud A- - ve Ga- - bri-
por- ta. Su- mens il- lud A- - ve
por- ta. Su- mens
por- ta. Su- mens il- lud
[tasto solo]
[5]

37
-e- lis o- - - - re, Fun-
Ga- bri- e- - lis o- - - - re,
il- lud A- - ve Ga- bri- e- lis o- re,
A- - ve Ga- bri- e- lis o- - re,
6 5 6 5 9 8

230

59
Mu- tans He- vae no- - -
He- vae no- - - - men, Mu- - tans
- men, Mu- tans He vae no- - men,
pa ce, Mu- tans He- vae no- -
66
-men, Mu- - tans He- - vae no- - men,
He- vae no- men, He- - vae no- men, Mu- tans
Mu- tans He- - vae, He- vae no- - -
-men, Mu- tans He- vae no- - -

73
He- vae no- - men.
He- - vae no- men. Mon- stra te
- men, no- - men. Mon- stra te es- se
- - - men.
[tasto solo]
81
Mon- stra te es- se ma- trem: Su- mat per te
es- se ma- trem: Su- mat per te pre- ces,
ma- trem, ma- trem: Su- mat per te pre- -
Mon- stra te es- se ma- trem: Su- mat per te pre- -
[5]

89
pre- ces, Qui pro no- bis na- tus,
Qui pro no- bis na- - - tus, Tu-
- ces, Qui pro no- bis na- - - tus,
-ces, Qui pro

95
Tu- lit es- se, es- - se tu- us.
-lit, tu- lit es- se tu- - us.
Tu- lit es- se tu- us. Vir- go sin- gu-
no- bis na- tus, Tu- lit es- se tu- us.
9 8
[tasto solo]

234

115
Nos cul- pis so- lu- tos,
cul- pis so- lu- - tos, Mi- tes fac et
Nos cul- pis so- lu- tos, Mi- tes
Nos cul- pis so- lu-
[tasto solo]
6
[♯]
121
Mi- tes fac et ca- - - stos.
ca- stos, Mi- tes fac et ca- - stos.
fac et ca- stos, et ca- - stos.
-tos, Mi- tes fac et ca- - stos.
[4]
[♯]
[♯]

128
Sit laus De- - o Pa- - tri,
Sit laus De- - o, De- o Pa- - tri,
Sit laus De- - o Pa- - tri,
Sit laus De- o Pa- - tri,
[♮6]
136
Sum- mo Chri- sto de- - cus, Sum- - mo
Sum- mo Chri- sto de- - cus,
Sum- mo
Sum- mo Chri- sto
[tasto solo]
[5]

142
Chri- sto de- - - - cus,
Sum- mo Chri- sto, Chri- sto de- - -
Chri- sto de- - cus, Sum- mo Chri- sto de-
de- - cus, de- - - -
9 8
149
Spi- ri- tu- i San- - - -
-[cus,] Spi- ri- tu- i San- cto, Spi-
-cus, Spi-
-cus,
[tasto solo]
[♯6]

156
- cto, San- - - - cto,
-ri- tu- i San- - - cto,
-ri- tu- i San- cto, Tri- bus
Spi- ri- tu- i San- cto, San-
[♯] [♭]
162
Tri- bus ho- nor,
Tri- bus ho- nor, ho- - - nor
ho- nor, ho- - nor u- nus, Tri- bus
- - - cto, Tri- bus

168
ho- - nor u- nus, Tri- - bus ho- - nor,
u- nus, ho- - nor u- nus, Tri- bus ho-
ho- - nor u- nus, ho- - nor u-
ho- nor, ho- nor u- nus, Tri- bus ho- nor
[♮]
175
ho- - - nor u- - nus.
- - nor, ho- nor u- - nus.
-nus, Tri- bus ho- nor u- - nus.
u- nus, ho- - nor u- - nus.

Jesu Redemptor omnium

*For this setting, the basso ripieno comprises violoncello, theorbo, bassoon, and double bass.

14
-nem, Pa- rem pa- ter- - nae
o- ri- gi- nem, Pa- rem pa- ter-
an- te o- ri- gi- nem,
lu- cis an- te o- ri- - gi- nem,
[tasto solo]
21
glo- - ri- ae, Pa- rem pa- ter-
- nae, pa- ter- - nae glo- ri- ae,
Pa- rem pa- ter- - nae glo- - ri-
Pa- rem pa- ter- - - nae
4 3

28
- nae glo- ri- ae, quem Pa- rem pa- ter- - - nae
Pa- rem pa- ter- - nae glo- ri- ae, Pa- rem
-ae, Pa- rem pa- ter-
glo- - ri- ae, Pa- rem pa-
7 ♮6
[tasto solo]
[5]
35
glo- - ri- ae, Pa- ter su- pre- mus, Pa- -
pa- ter- nae glo- ri- ae, Pa- - - ter,
- nae, pa- ter- nae glo- - ri- ae,
-ter- - nae glo- - ri- ae,
[♮]
[tasto solo]

243

56
- ter - su- pre- mus e- - di- dit.
- ter su- pre- mus e- - di- dit.
-pre- mus, su- pre- mus e- - di- dit.
su- pre- - mus e- - di- dit.
[♮4]
2
63
Me- men- to,
Me- men- to, re- rum Con- di- tor, me- men- to, No- stri quod
Me- men- to, re- rum Con- di- tor, re- - rum Con-
Me- men- to, re- rum
[tasto solo]
[5]

71
re- rum Con- di- tor, No- stri quod o- - lim cor- po-
o- lim cor- - - po- ris, Sa- cra- ta
- di- tor, No- stri quod o- lim cor- po- ris, Sa-
Con- di- tor, re- rum Con- di- tor, No- stri quod o- lim
[♯]
78
-ris, Sa- cra- ta ab al- vo, ab al- vo Vir-
ab al- - - vo, ab al- vo Vir- - gi-
-cra- ta ab al- vo Vir- gi- nis Na- - scen- do,
cor- po- ris, Sa- cra- ta ab al- vo Vir- gi- nis Na-

-ginis Na-scen-do, for- mam sum-pse- ris.
-nis Na- scen- do, for- mam sum- pse- ris. Te-
for- mam, na- scen- do, for- mam sum- pse- [ris.]
-scen- do, for- mam sum- pse- [ris.]

[tasto solo]

-sta- tur hoc prae- sens, prae- sens, prae-
Te- sta- tur hoc praes- sens di- es, prae- sens,
Te- sta- tur hoc prae- sens
Te- sta- tur hoc

247

114
-lus e si- nu Pa- tris Mun- di sa- - lus ad- ve-
Pa- tris Mun- di sa- - lus ad- ve-
Pa- - tris Mun- di sa- - lus ad- ve-
e si- - nu Pa- tris Mun- di sa- lus ad- ve-
121
- ne- ris. Je- - su, ti- bi, ti- bi sit glo-
- ne- ris. Je- su, ti- bi sit glo-
- ne- ris. Je- - su, ti- bi, ti- bi sit
- ne- ris. Je- - su, ti- bi sit

129
-ri- a, Qui na- tus es de Vir- - gi- ne, de
- ri- a, Qui na- tus es de Vir- - gi-
glo- ri- a, Qui
glo- ri- a,
[tasto solo]
[5]
136
Vir- gi- ne, Cum Pa- tre et
-ne, de Vir- - gi- ne, Cum Pa-
na- tus es de Vir- - gi- ne,
Qui na- tus es de Vir- gi- ne, de Vir- gi- ne,
7 ♮6
[tasto solo]

143
al- - mo Spi- ri- tu, Cum Pa-
-tre et al- mo, et al- - mo Spi- ri- tu,
Cum Pa- tre et al- mo Spi-
Cum Pa- tre et al-
[5]
150
-tre et al- mo Spi- ri- tu, Cum Pa- tre, cum Pa- -
Cum Pa- tre et al- mo Spi- ri- tu, Cum
- ri- tu, Cum Pa-
- mo Spi- - ri- tu, Cum
7 ♮6
[tasto solo]
[5]

157
-tre et al- mo Spi- ri- tu, In sem- pi- ter- na, in
Pa- tre et al- mo Spi- ri- tu, In sem-
-tre et al- mo, et al- - mo Spi- ri- tu,
Pa- trc ct al- - mo Spi- - ri- tu,
[tasto solo]
164
sem- - pi- ter- na sae- - cu- la,
- pi- ter- - - na sae- - cu- la, In
In sem- - pi- ter- na, sem- pi-
In sem- - - pi-
[5]

171
In sem- - pi- ter- na sae- cu- la, In
sem- - pi- ter- na sae- - cu- la, In sem- pi-
-ter- na sae- - cu- la, In sem- - pi-
-ter- na sae- cu- la, In sem-
178
sem- - pi- ter- na sae- - cu- la.
-ter- - na sae- - - cu- la.
-ter- - na, sem- pi- ter- na sae- cu- la.
- - pi- ter- na sae- - cu- la.

Marian Antiphons

Alma Redemptoris Mater

*The parts of oboe 1, oboe 2, and bassoon were added later (exact date unknown) in a hand other than Heinichen's and are optional in performance.

†The somewhat idiosyncratic dynamic markings of the source viola part have been retained.

5
p assai
Ma- ter, Ma- ter, al- - ma Re- dem- pto- - ris, Re- dem- pto-
solo
Al- ma Re- dem- pto- ris Ma- ter, al- ma Re- dem- pto- ris Ma- ter,
solo
Al- ma Re- dem- pto- ris Ma- ter, al- ma Re- dem- pto-
solo
Al- ma
6
p

8
poco p
[poco] p
[poco] p
- ris, al- ma Re- dem- pto- - ris Ma- ter, quae per- vi- a cae- li
Re- dem- pto- ris Ma- ter, al- ma Re- dem- pto- ris Ma- ter, quae per- vi- a cae- li
- ris Ma- ter, al- ma Re- dem- pto- ris Ma- ter,
Re- dem- pto- ris Ma- ter, al- ma Re- dem- pto- ris Ma- ter,

258

porta manes, Et stella maris, et stella maris,

porta manes, Et stella maris, et stella maris,

tutti
succurre cadenti surgere qui

suc- cur- re ca-den- ti sur- ge- re qui cu- rat, qui

suc- cur- re ca-den- ti sur- ge- re qui cu- rat, sur- ge- re qui

suc- cur- re ca-den- ti sur- ge- re qui cu- rat, sur- ge- re qui cu- rat, qui

cu- rat po- pu- lo, suc- cur- re ca-den- ti sur- ge- re qui

17
cu- rat po- pu- lo, qui cu- rat, sur- ge- re, sur- ge- re qui cu- rat po- pu-
cu- rat po- pu- lo, qui cu- rat, sur- ge- re qui cu- rat po- pu-
cu- rat po- pu- lo, qui cu- rat, sur- ge- re qui cu- rat, cu- rat po- pu-
cu- rat po- pu- lo, qui cu- rat, sur- ge- re qui cu- rat po- pu-

20
p assai
p assai
[solo]
-lo: Tu quae ge- nu- i- sti, quae
solo
-lo: Tu quae ge- nu- i- sti, quae ge- nu- i-
[solo]
-lo: Tu quae ge- nu- i-
[solo]
-lo: Tu quae

ge- nu- i- sti, na- tu- ra, na- tu- ra mi- ran- te, tu- um san- ctum, san-ctum Ge-

-sti, quae ge- nu- i- sti, na- tu- ra, na- tu- ra mi- ran- te, tu- um san-ctum, san- ctum Ge-

-sti, ge- nu- i- sti, na- tu- ra, na- tu- ra mi- ran- te, tu- um san- ctum, san- ctum

ge- nu- i- sti, na- tu- ra, na- tu- ra mi- ran- te, tu- um san- ctum, san-ctum Ge- ni-

-nitorem: Virgo prius ac posterius,

[soli] -nitorem: Virgo prius ac posterius,

Genitorem:

-torem:

solo
Gabrielis ab ore sumens illud A-

32
f
f
f
f
f
[tutti]
pec- ca- to- rum mi- se- re- - re, mi- se- re-
[tutti]
pec- ca- to- rum mi- se- re- re, pec- ca- to- rum mi- se- re-
tutti
-ve, pec- ca- to- rum mi- se- re- re, pec- ca- to- rum mi- se- re- re, mi- se-
[tutti]
pec- ca- to- rum mi- se- re- re, pec- ca- to- rum mi- se- re- re,
f
f
6 7 6 6 5
f

36
- re, mi- se- re- re, mi- se- re-
-re, mi- se- re- re, mi- se- re- -
-re- re, mi- se- re- re, mi- se- re- re, mi- se- re- re,
mi- se- re- re, mi- se- re- - re, mi- se- re- re, mi- se- re-
6 ♭5 9 8 ♭ 6 9 8 ♭4 3 7 7 ♭ ♭7 7 7 6 5

40
- re, mi- se- re- re, mi- se- re- re, pec- ca- to- rum
- re, mi- se- re- - re, mi- se- re- re, pec- ca- to- rum
mi- se- re- re, mi- se- re- re, mi- se- re- re, pec- ca- to- rum
- re, mi- se- re- re,

44
f
p
f
f assai
solo
[solo]
[tutti]
tutti
mi- se- re- - - - re, mi- se-
mi- se- re- - - - re, mi- se-
mi- se- re- re, mi- se- re- re, mi- se-
mi- se- re- re, mi- se-

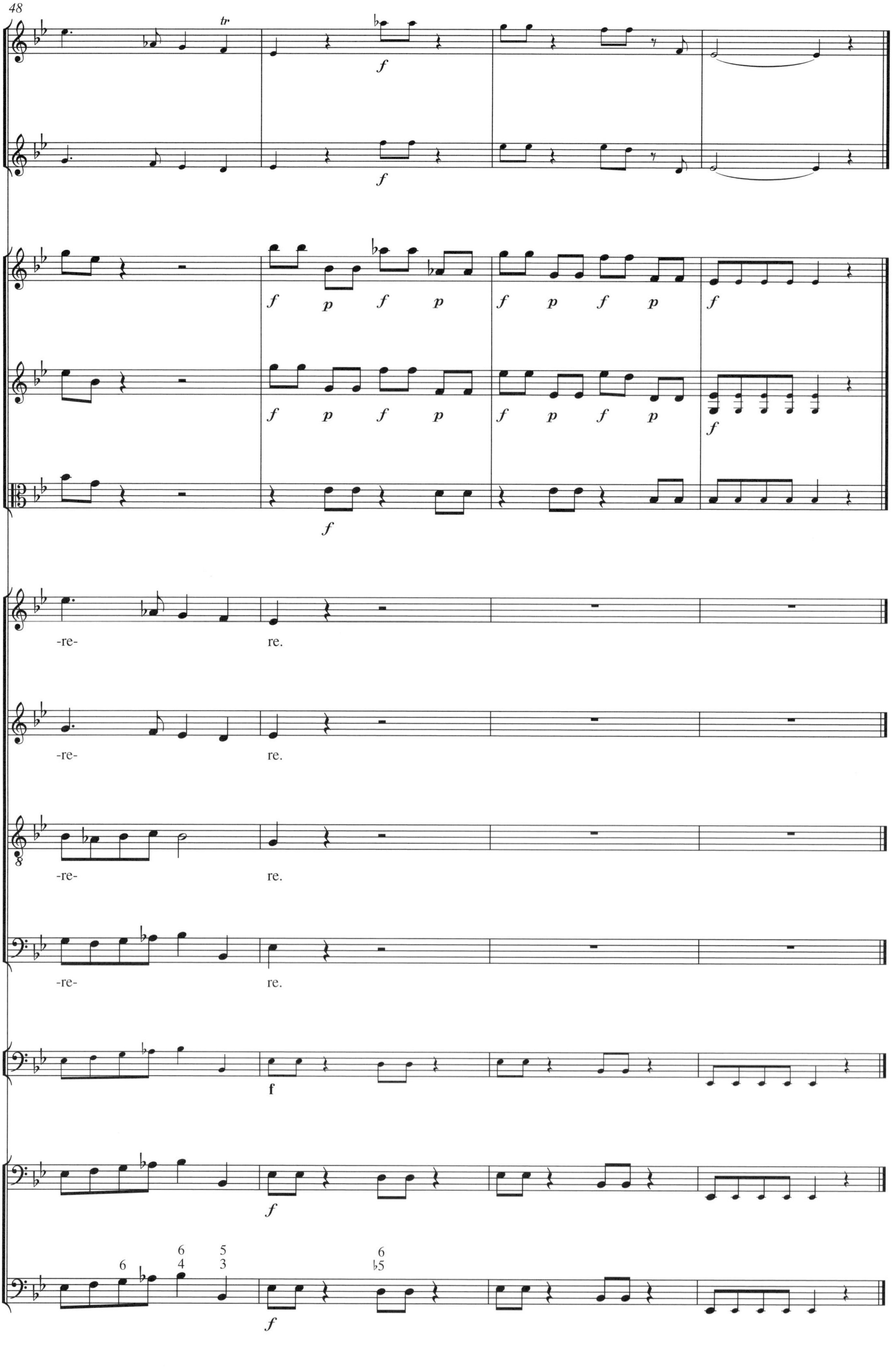
48
-re-
re.
-re-
re.
-re-
re.
-re-
re.

Ave Regina

1. Ave Regina

8
An- ge- lo- rum: Sal- ve — ra- dix, sal- ve — por- ta, Ex qua mun- do — lux est — or-
11
- ta, est or- ta,
A- ve Re- gi- na, Re-

14
-gi- na cae- lo- rum, A- ve Do- mi- na An- ge- lo- rum: Sal- ve ra- dix, sal-ve
17
por- ta, Sal-ve ra- dix, sal- ve por- ta, Ex qua mun- do lux est or- ta, est or-

-ta, Sal- ve por- ta, sal- ve ra- dix, sal- ve por- ta, Ex quo mun- do lux est or-

-ta.

2. Gaude Virgo gloriosa

8
Gau- de Vir- go glo- ri- o- sa,
Su- per om- nes spe- ci- o- sa,
12
Gau- de Vir- go glo- ri- o- - - sa, Su- per

16
soli
soli
om-nes spe-ci- o- sa,
20
tutti
tutti
Gau- de Vir- go glo-ri- o- sa,

276

36
Ob. 1
Ob. 2
Vn. 1
Vn. 2
Va.
S solo
D.r.
B.c.
soli
soli
glo- ri- o- sa, Su- per om- nes spe- ci- o- sa.
40
[tutti]
[tutti]

3. Vale

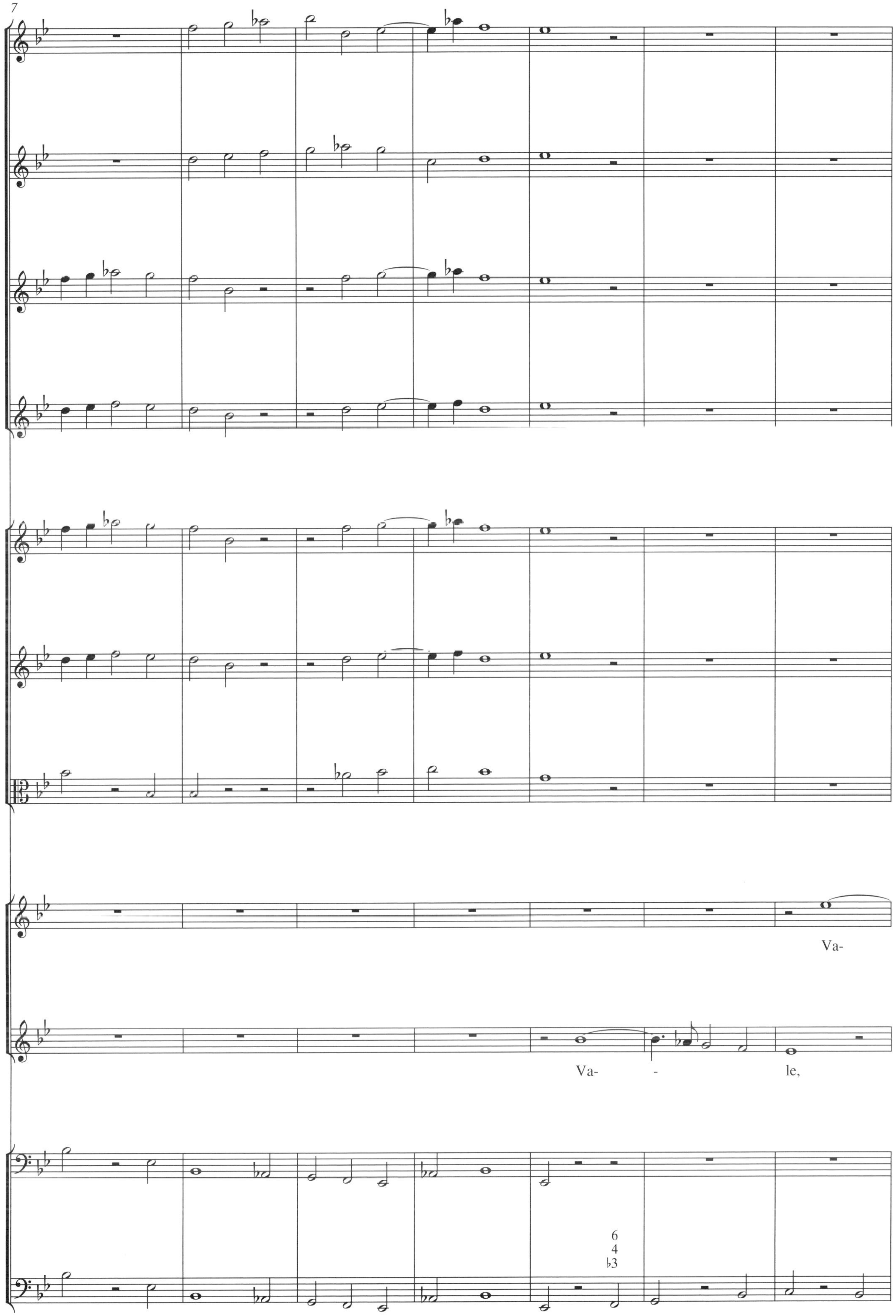
7
Va-
Va- - le,
6
4
♭3

14
Fl. 1
Fl. 2
Vn. 1
Vn. 2
Va.
S solo
- le, vale, o valde, o valde decora, Et pro
A solo
vale, vale, o valde, o valde decora,
B.r.
B.c.
21
Fl. 1
Fl. 2
Vn. 1
Vn. 2
S solo
nobis Christum exora,
A solo
Et pro nobis Christum exora,
B.r.
B.c.

28
Fl. 1
Fl. 2
Ob. 1
Ob. 2
Vn. 1
Vn. 2
Va.
p
S solo
Va- le, va- le, o val- de, o val- de de- co- ra,
A solo
Va- le, va- le, o val- - de de- co- ra, Et pro
B.r.
B.c.
35
Fl. 1
Fl. 2
Vn. 1
Vn. 2
Va.
S solo
Et pro no- - - bis Chri- stum ex- o- ra,
A solo
no- - bis, pro no- - bis Chri- stum ex- o- ra,
B.c.

41
Fl. 1
Fl. 2
Ob. 1
Ob. 2
Vn. 1
Vn. 2
Va.
S solo
Chri- stum ex- o- -
A solo
Chri- stum ex- o- - -
B.r.
B.c.
47
Fl. 1
Fl. 2
Vn. 1
Vn. 2
Va.
S solo
- - - - - ra,
A solo
- - - - - ra,
B.c.

283

Regina caeli in G

1. Regina caeli

285

10
Fl. 1
Fl. 2
Ob. 1
Ob. 2
Vn. 1
Vn. 2
Va.
A
solo
Re- gi- na cae- li lae-
B.r.
B.c.
14
Fl. 1
Fl. 2
Vn. 1
Vn. 2
Va.
A
-ta- re, lae- ta- - re, lae- ta-
B.c.

17
p
p
p
- - re, lae- ta- re, Re-
20
Vn. 1
Vn. 2
Va.
A
-gi- na cae- li lae- ta- re, al- - - le- lu-
B.c.

24
Fl. 1
Fl. 2
Ob. 1
Ob. 2
Vn. 1
f
Vn. 2
f
Va.
f
S
[tutti]
Re- gi- na cae- li lae- ta- re, lae- ta- -
A
[tutti]
-ia, Re- gi- na cae- li lae- ta- re, lae- ta- - re, lae- ta-
T
[tutti]
Re- gi- na cae- li lae- ta- re, lae- ta- re,
B
[tutti]
Re- gi- na cae- li lae- ta- re, lae- ta-
B.r.
B.c.

27
- re, lae- ta- - re, al- le- lu-
-re, lae- ta- - re, lae- ta- re, al- le- lu-
lae- ta- re, lae- ta- re, lae- ta- re, al- le- lu-
- re, lae- ta- - - re, al- le- lu-

30
tr
-ia, lae- ta- re, lae- ta- re,
-ia, lae- ta- re, lae- ta- re,
-ia, lae- ta- re, lae- ta- re,
-ia, lae- ta- re, lae- ta- re,

Re-

36
Ob. 1
Ob. 2
Vn. 1
Vn. 2
Va.
A
B.r.
B.c.
p
-gi- na cae- li lae- ta- re, lae- ta- -
40
- - re, lae- ta- re, Re- gi- na cae- li lae- ta-
44
più p
- re, al- le- lu- ia, lae- ta- re, Re- gi- na cae- li lae- ta-

48
Fl. 1
Fl. 2
Ob. 1
Ob. 2
Vn. 1
f
Vn. 2
f
Va.
f
S
[tutti]
Re- gi- na cae- li lae- ta- re,
A
re, al- le- lu- ia, Re- gi- na cae- li lae- ta- re,
[tutti]
T
[tutti]
Re- gi- na cae- li lae- ta- re,
B
[tutti]
Re- gi- na cae- li lae- ta- re,
B.r.
B.c.

51
lae- ta- - re, lae- ta-
lae- ta- re, lae- ta- - re, lae- ta-
lae- ta- re, lae- ta- re, lae- ta-
lae- ta- - re,

54
- re, lae- ta- - - re, al- le-
-re, lae- ta- - re, lae- ta- re, lae- ta- re, al- le-
- re, lae- ta- re, lae- ta- re, lae- ta- re, al- le-
lae- ta- - - re, al- le-
6
5 6 6

57
tr
pp
-lu- ia, Re- gi- na cae- li lae- ta- re.
-lu- ia, Re- gi- na cae- li lae- ta- re.
-lu- ia, Re- gi- na cae- li lae- ta- re.
-lu- ia, Re- gi- na cae- li lae- ta- re.

297

2. Quia quem meruisti

*An instruction for the violin to double the voice was added at a later time in Heinichen's hand.

13
al-
16
Ob. 1
Ob. 2
Ob. 3
Vn. 1
T solo
B.c.
tr
6
19
Ob. 1
Ob. 2
Ob. 3
Bn.
Vn. 1
T solo
le- lu- ia, al- le- lu- [ia,]
B.c.

qui- a quem me- ru- i- sti por- ta- re, al- le- lu- ia: Re- sur- re-

36
Ob. 1
Ob. 2
Ob. 3
Bn.
Vn. 1
T solo
-xit, al- le- lu- ia, re- sur- re- -
B.c.
40
Vn. 1
T solo
- - -xit, al- le- lu-
B.c.
43
Ob. 1
Ob. 2
Ob. 3
Bn.
Vn. 1
T solo
-ia.
B.c.

3. Ora pro nobis

303

16
-[ra,]
o- ra, o-
o- ra, o-
19
Vn. 1, 2
Va.
S solo
-ra, o- ra pro no-
A solo
-ra, o- ra pro no- bis
B.c.
22
Fl. 1
Fl. 2
Vn. 1, 2
Va.
S solo
-bis De- um,
A solo
De- um, o- ra, o-
B.c.

25
o- ra, o-
-ra, o- ra, o-
28
Vn. 1, 2
Va.
S solo
-ra pro no- -
A solo
-ra, o- - ra pro
B.c.
31
- - bis De-
no- - - bis De-

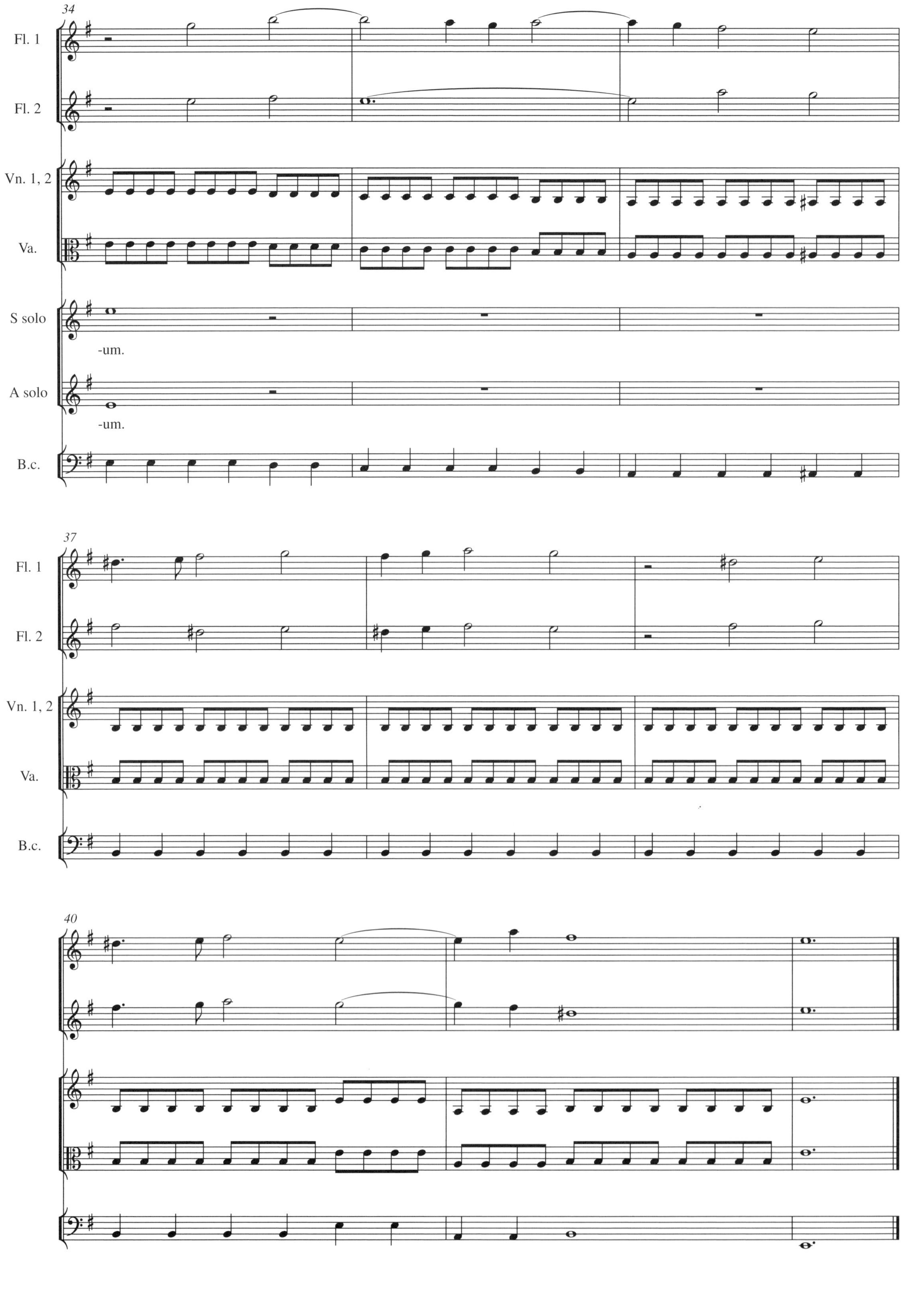
34
Fl. 1
Fl. 2
Vn. 1, 2
Va.
S solo
-um.
A solo
-um.
B.c.
37
Fl. 1
Fl. 2
Vn. 1, 2
Va.
B.c.
40

4. Alleluia

*For this movement, the basso ripieno comprises violoncello, theorbo, bassoon, and double bass.

4
-lu- ia, al- le- lu- ia, al- -
-ia, al- le- lu- ia, al- le- lu- ia, al- le- - lu- ia, al- le-
[tutti]
Al- le- lu- ia, al- - le- lu- ia, al- le- lu- ia, al- le-
[tutti]
Al- le- lu- ia, al-
[5]

8
- le- lu- ia, al- le- lu- ia,
-lu- ia, al- le- lu- ia, al- le- lu- ia,
-lu- ia, al- le- lu- ia, al- - le- lu- ia,
- le- lu- ia, al- le- lu- ia,
6 7

12
al- le- - lu- ia, al- le- lu- ia,
al- le- lu- ia, al- le- lu- ia, al-
al- le- - lu- ia,
[al- le- lu- ia, al- le- lu- ia,]
[tasto solo]

16
al- le- lu- ia, al- le- - lu- ia, al- le-
- le- lu- ia, al- [le]- - lu- ia, al- le- lu- ia,
al- le- lu- ia, al- - le- lu- ia,
al- le- lu- ia, al- le- lu- ia,
[5]
[tasto solo]

20
-lu- ia, al- - le- lu- ia, al- le- lu- ia, al- le-
al- le- lu- ia, al- le- lu- ia, al- le-
al- le- lu- ia, al- le- lu- ia,
al- le- lu- ia, al-
[♯]

313

27
- lu- ia, al- le- lu- ia, al- le- lu-
- lu- ia, al- le- lu- ia, al- le- lu-
- - le- lu- ia, al- le-
al- le- lu- ia, al- le- lu- ia,

30
p
-ia, al- le- lu- ia, al- le- - lu-
-ia, al- le- lu- ia, al- le- - lu-
-lu- ia, al- le- lu- ia, al- -
al- le- lu- ia, al- le- lu- ia,

33
-ia, al- le- lu- ia, al- le- lu- ia, al- le- lu- ia, al- le- lu- ia.
-ia, al- le- lu- ia, al- le- lu- ia, al- le- lu- ia, al- le- lu- ia.
- le- lu- ia, al- le- lu- ia, al- le- lu- ia, al- le- lu- ia.
al- le- lu- ia, al- le- lu- ia, al- le- lu- ia, al- le- lu- ia.

Regina caeli in D

1. Regina caeli

7
Ob. 1
Ob. 2
Vn. 1
p
Vn. 2
p
Va.
p
A solo
Re- gi- na cae- li lae- ta- - re, lae- ta- -
B.r.
B.c.
11
Vn. 1
Vn. 2
Va.
A solo
- - - re, lae- ta-
B.r.
B.c.
14
- - - re, al- le- lu-

17
Ob. 1
Ob. 2
Vn. 1
Vn. 2
Va.
f
p
S
tutti
Re- gi- na cae- li lae- ta- re,
A
[tutti]
Re- gi- na cae- li lae- ta- re, lae- ta- re,
T
[tutti]
Re- gi- na cae- li lae- ta- [re,]
B
[tutti]
Re- gi- na cae- li lae- ta- re, lae- ta- re,
A solo
-ia, Re- gi- na cae- li lae- ta- - re, lae-
B.r.
B.c.
21
Vn. 1
Vn. 2
Va.
A solo
-ta- - - re,
B.r.
B.c.

24
al- - -
27
Ob. 1
Ob. 2
Vn. 1
f p p
Vn. 2
f p p
Va.
f
S
al- le- lu- ia, al- le- lu- ia,
A
al- le- lu- ia, al- le- lu- ia,
T
al- le- lu- ia, al- le- lu- ia,
B
al- le- lu- ia, al- le- lu- ia,
A solo
- le- lu- ia, lae- ta- -
B.r.
B.c.

31
f
f
f
p
f
p
p
f
p
al- le- lu- ia, al- le-lu- ia,
al- le- lu- ia, al- le- lu- ia,
al- le- lu- ia, al- le-lu- ia,
al- le- lu- ia, al- le-lu- ia,
- - re, al- -

35
Re- gi- na cae- li lae- ta- re, al-
Re- gi- na cae- li lae- ta- re, lae- ta- re, al-
Re- gi- na cae- li lae- ta- re, al-
Re- gi- na cae- li lae- ta- re, lae- ta- re, al-
- - le- lu- ia.

323

2. Quia quem meruisti

*For this movement, the basso ripieno comprises violoncello, theorbo, bassoon, and double bass.

325

16
-ia, al- le- - lu- ia, al- le- lu- ia,
-le- lu- ia, qui- a quem me- ru- i- sti por-
me- ru- i- sti por- ta- re, por- ta- re, al- le- lu- ia, al-
- re, al- - - - le- lu-
7 6
20
qui- a quem me- ru- i- sti por- ta- -
-ta- re, por- ta- re, al- le- lu- ia, al- le- lu-
-le- - lu- ia, al- -
-ia, al- le- lu- ia, al- -

24
-re, al- le- lu- ia, al- le- - lu- ia,
-ia, al- le- lu- ia, qui- a quem
-le- lu- ia, al- le- lu- ia, al- le- lu- ia, al-
- le- lu- ia, al- - le- lu-
28
qui- a quem me- ru- i- sti por- ta-
me- ru- i- sti por- ta- re, por- ta- re, al- le- lu-
- le- lu- ia, al- le- lu- ia,
-ia, qui- a quem me- ru-

32
- re, al- le- lu- ia, al- le- lu- ia,
-ia, al- le- - lu- ia, al- le- lu- ia, al-
qui- a quem me- ru- i- sti por- ta- - re, por- ta-
-i- sti por- ta- - re, al- - - le-
7 6
36
qui- a quem me- ru- i- sti por- ta- - re, al- le- lu- ia, al-
-le- lu- ia, al- - le- lu- ia, al- le-
- re, al- le- - lu- ia, al- le- lu- ia, al- le-
- lu- ia, al- le- lu- ia, qui- a quem me- ru-
5 6
9 8

3. Resurrexit sicut dixit

5
Re- sur-
9
Vn. 1, 2
Va.
T solo
B.c.
p
-re- xit, re- sur- re- xit, sic- ut di- xit, re- sur-
13
-re- - - -

17
Ob. 1, 2
Vn. 1, 2
f
Va.
T solo
- - - xit, re- sur- re- xit, sic- ut
B.r.
B.c.
21
T solo
di- xit, al- le- lu- ia,
B.c.
25
Ob. 1, 2
Vn. 1, 2
Va.
T solo
al- le- lu- ia,
B.r.
B.c.

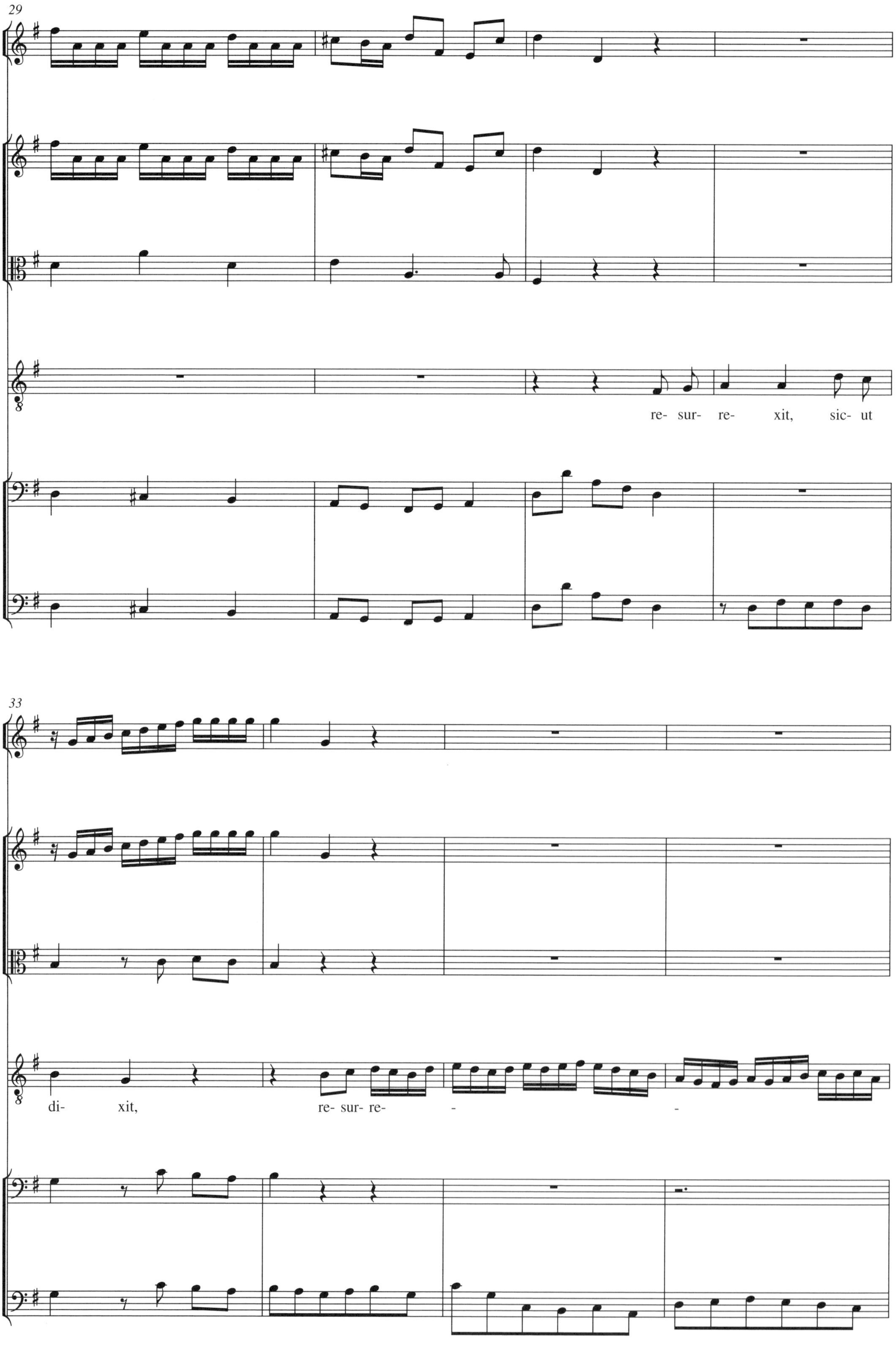
29
re- sur- re- xit, sic- ut
33
di- xit, re- sur- re- - -

re- sur- re- xit, sic- ut di- xit, al- le- lu- ia,

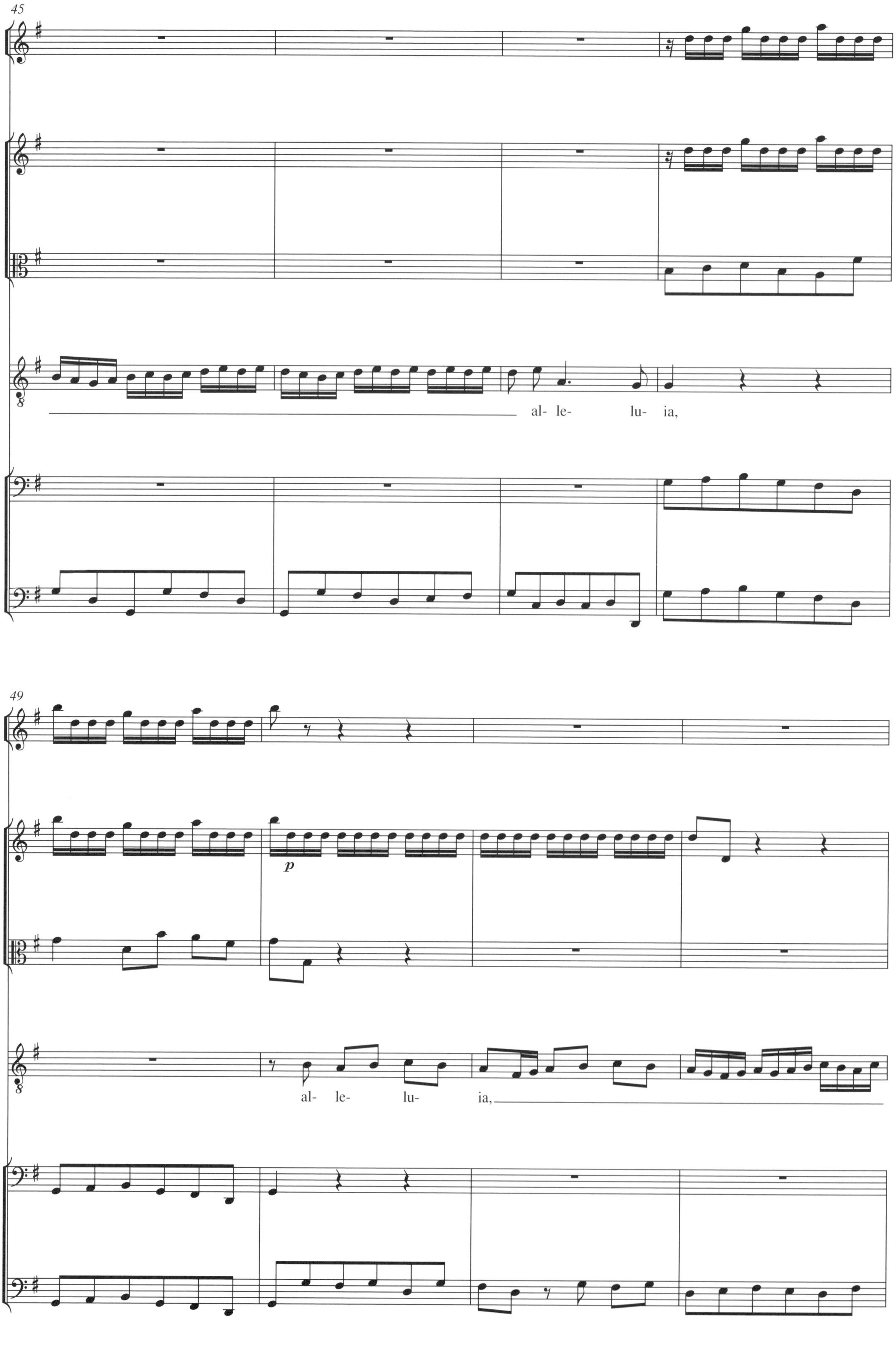
45
al- le- lu- ia,
49
p
al- le- lu- ia,

335

4. Ora pro nobis

5. Alleluia

10
Ob. 1
Ob. 2
Vn. 1
p
Vn. 2
p
Va.
A solo
Al- le- lu- ia, al- le- lu- ia,
B.r.
B.c.
15
Vn. 1
Vn. 2
Va.
p
A solo
al- le- lu- ia,
B.r.
B.c.
20
al- le- lu- ia,

al- le- lu- ia,

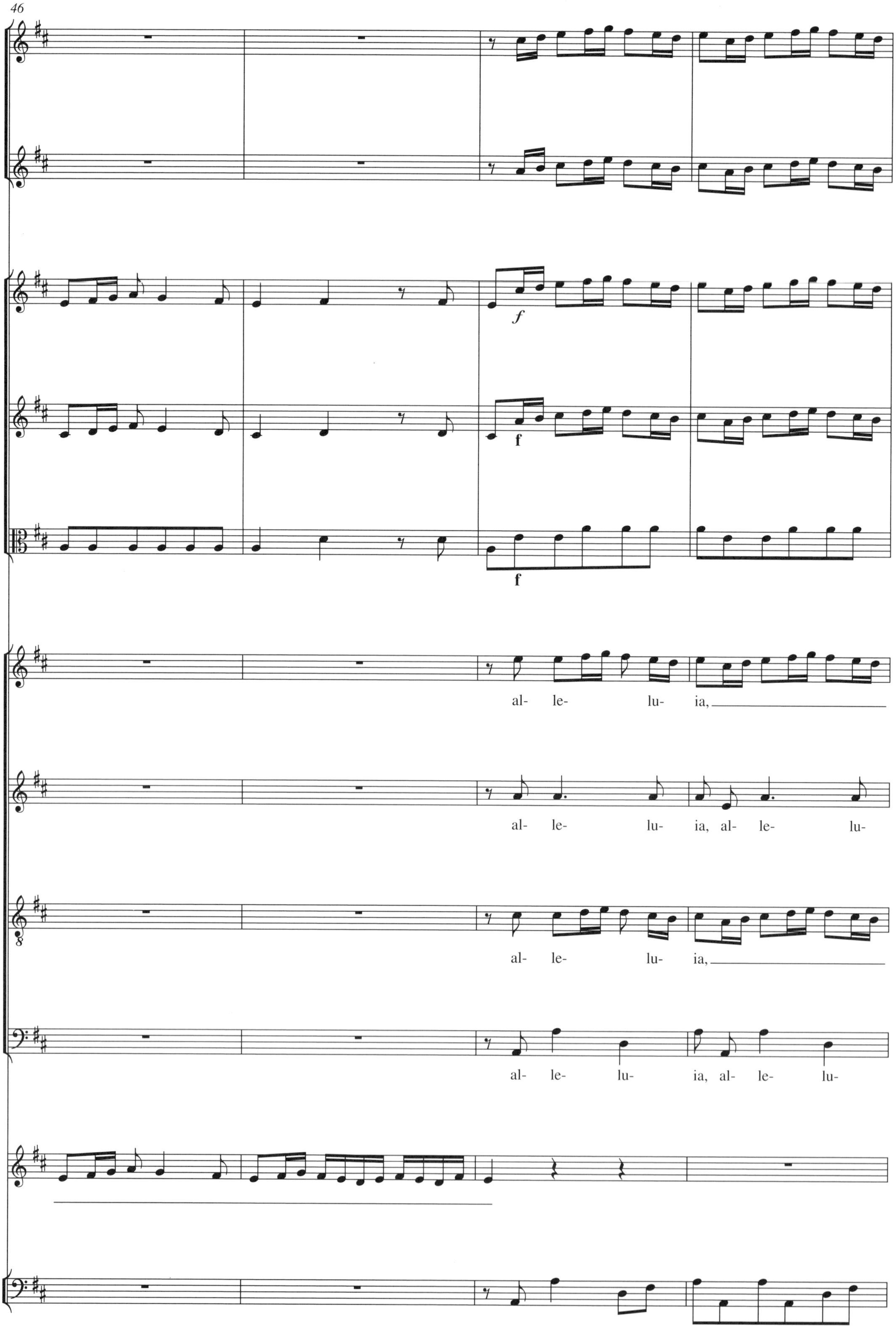
46
f
f
f
al- le- lu- ia,
al- le- lu- ia, al- le- lu-
al- le- lu- ia,
al- le- lu- ia, al- le- lu-

-ia, -ia, al- - - -

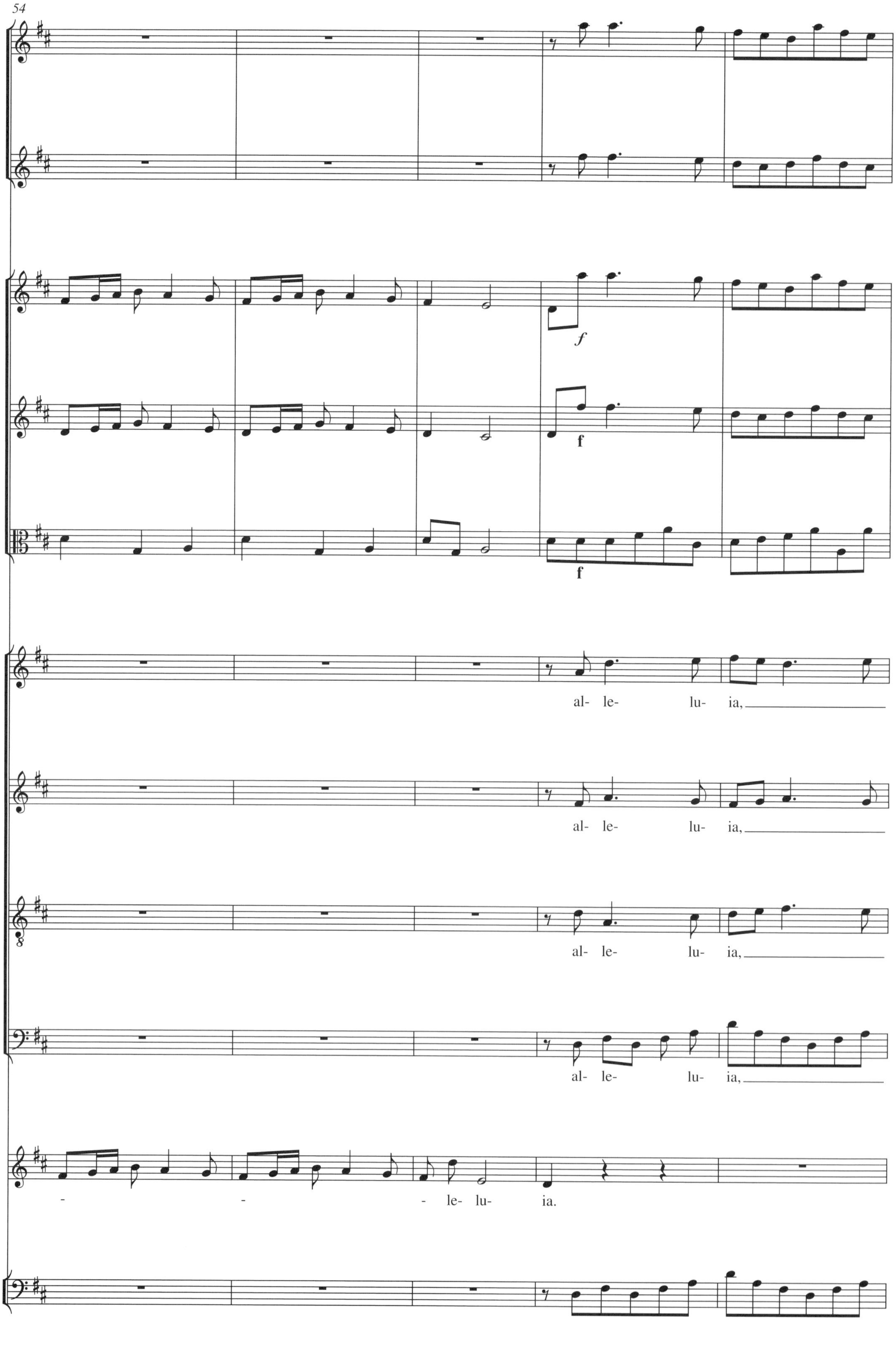
54
f
f
f
al- le- lu- ia,
al- le- lu- ia,
al- le- lu- ia,
al- le- lu- ia,
- - - le- lu- ia.

59
— al- le- lu- ia, al- le- - lu- ia.
— al- le- lu- ia, al- le- - lu- ia.
— al- le- lu- ia, al- le- lu- ia, al- le- lu- ia.
— al- le- lu- ia, al- le- - lu- ia.

Critical Report

Sources

All the sources for this edition are sole sources held in the Sächsische Landesbibliothek – Staats- und Universitätsbibliothek, Dresden (D-Dlb). They are all in quarto landscape format, bound between marbled boards dating from the middle of the eighteenth century.

The shelf mark of each source is listed below, together with the size, binding details, and any additional text such as titles, part names, dates, and measure counts. Such additional text is autograph, unless otherwise stated. The system layout is also described, using the abbreviations for voices and instruments used in this edition.

Many of the sources also contain cataloguing data, added at various stages over the course of the eighteenth century as the Hofkapelle's music collection was reorganized; this data is not listed explicitly.

All the sources apart from one, the *Alma Redemptoris Mater*, are autograph.

Beatus vir

D-Dlb Mus. 2398-D-44, size 315 x 230 mm, bound in one gathering of two bifolia plus one bifolio (twelve pages). The first page contains the title text: "Beatus Vir [with "2dum" inserted beneath] à 2 Voci con 2 Flaut. Travers. ò 2 Hautbois soli. di Giov. Heinichen". The pages are numbered and ruled with ten staves. The setting is in a single movement on pages 1–11. A measure count and the date "Mens Maij 1724" are at the end of page 11.

Source layout is two five-stave systems per page: Fl. or Ob. 1, Fl. or Ob. 2, A solo, T solo, B.c. Source part names are "Alto", "Tenore".

Confitebor tibi Domine

D-Dlb Mus. 2398-D-40, size 315 x 223 mm, bound in one gathering of two bifolia (eight pages). The first page contains the title text: "Confitebor à 4. di S. Giov. Heinichen". The pages are numbered and ruled with ten staves. The setting is in a single movement on pages 1–6. The date "Mense Maij 1727" appears at the left of page 6.

Source layout is two five-stave systems per page: S / Vn. 1 / Ob. 1 / Ob. 2, A / Vn. 2, T / Va., B, B.c. Source part names are "Viol. i / Hautb. 1 e 2", "Violin 2", "Violetta".

Dixit Dominus

D-Dlb Mus. 2398-D-37, size 320 x 235 mm. The binding is rather damaged, so it is not possible to determine the gatherings (twenty-two pages). The first page contains the title text: "Dixit [with "4tum" inserted beneath] à 4. voc. con strom. di. Giov. Heinichen". The pages are numbered and ruled with ten staves. The setting is in a single movement on pages 1–21. The date "Mense Aprilj 1726 / Finis" appears at the right of page 21. Associated with the score is a non-autograph instrumental "Basso" part, on a single sheet, 221 x 320 mm.

Source layout is one ten-stave system per page: Ob. 1, Ob. 2, Vn. 1, Vn. 2, Va, S, A, T, B, B.c. Source part names are "Hautbois", "Violini".

In exitu Israel

D-Dlb Mus. 2398-D-47, size 305 x 268 mm, bound in three gatherings of two bifolia (twenty-four pages). The first page contains the non-autograph title text: "P113. In Exitu Israel". The pages are numbered and ruled with thirteen staves. The setting is in five movements: "In exitu Israel," pages 1–7; "Non nobis Domine," pages 8–9; "Simulacra gentium," pages 9–12; "Domus Israel," pages 12–18; and "Gloria," pages 19–22. The word "Finis" appears at the bottom of page 22.

1. IN EXITU ISRAEL

Source layout on first page is one seven-stave system: Vn. 1 / Vn. 2 / Va., S, A, T, B, Bn. / Vc., B.c.; second and subsequent pages have one six-stave system per page: Ob. 1 / Ob. 2 / Vn. 1 / Vn. 2 / Va., S, A, T, B, B.c. Source part names are "Violini e Violette Unis", "Bassoni e Violone", "Organo".

2. NON NOBIS DOMINE

Source layout is three four-stave systems per page: S solo, A solo, T solo, B.c. Source part name is "Organo".

3. SIMULACRA GENTIUM

Source layout is one eight-stave system per page: Ob. 1 / Vn. 1, Ob. 2 / Vn. 2, Va., S, A, T, B, B.c. There are no source part names.

4. Domus Israel

Source layout is three four-stave systems per page: Ob. 1 / Ob. 2 / Vn. 1 / Vn. 2, Va., S solo / T solo / B solo, B.c. Source part names are "Canto, Tenore e Basso".

5. Gloria

Source layout is one eight-stave system per page: Ob. 1 / Vn. 1, Ob. 2 / Vn. 2, Va., S, A, T, B, B.c. There are no source part names.

Laetatus sum

D-Dlb Mus. 2398-D-33, size 312 x 235 mm, bound in eight gatherings of two bifolia (sixty-four pages). The pages are numbered and ruled with ten staves. This source contains four settings: *Laudate pueri*, *Laetatus sum*, *Nisi Dominus*, and *Lauda Jerusalem*. There is a loose title page (300 x 190 mm) containing the text: "1. Laudate pueri. / 2. Laetatus sum. / 3. Nisi dominus. / 4. Lauda Jerusalem", and to the right is: "Pro festis B.V.M". The setting of *Laetatus sum* occupies pages 16–33 of the source. At the end of the setting is the instruction "Siegue Nisi Dominus".

Source layout is one eight-stave system per page: Hn. 1, Hn. 2, Ob. 1 / Vn. 1, Ob. 2 / Vn. 2, Va., A solo, T solo, B.c. Source part names are "Corni da caccia", "à2 A. T."

Lauda Jerusalem

D-Dlb Mus. 2398-D-33, as described under *Laetatus sum* above. The first page of the setting contains the title text: "Lauda Jerusalem à 4 Voci". The setting occupies pages 48–65 of the source. The date "Xbr. 1726" is at the end of page 65.

Source layout is one ten-stave system per page: Hn. 1, Hn. 2, Ob. 1 / Vn. 1, Ob. 2 / Vn. 2, Va., S, A, T, B, B.c. Source part name is "Corni da caccia".

Laudate pueri

D-Dlb Mus. 2398-D-33, as described under *Laetatus sum* above. The first page of the setting contains the title text: "Laudate pueri (di Heinichen)". The setting occupies pages 1–15 of the source.

Source layout is one eight-stave system per page: Ob. 1 / Vn. 1, Ob. 2 / Vn. 2, Va., S, A, T, B, B.c. There are no source part names.

Nisi Dominus

D-Dlb Mus. 2398-D-33, as described under *Laetatus sum* above. The first page of the setting contains the title text: "Nisi Dominus à 2 Voci". The setting occupies pages 34–47 of the source.

Source layout is one seven-stave system per page: Ob. solo, Vn. 1, Vn. 2, Va., S solo, B solo, B.c. Source part names are "Hautb. Solo", "Violini (Senza Hautb.)", "Soprano", "Basso".

Magnificat in G

D-Dlb Mus. 2398-D-20, size 310 x 225 mm., bound in probably four gatherings of two bifolia (thirty-two pages). The binding is very fragile and the first page is torn. The title text on the first page is: "Magnificat (6tum) à 4 Voc. Con strom: di Giov. Heinichen". The setting is in six movements: "Magnificat," pages 1–5; "Quia respexit," pages 6–9; "Fecit potentiam," pages 9–17; "Suscepit Israel," pages 18–21; "Gloria," page 22; and "Sicut erat in principio," pages 23–29. All pages are numbered and ruled with ten staves. The date "Mens Martz / 1727." appears to the bottom right of page 32.

1. Magnificat

Source layout is one ten-stave system per page: Ob. 1, Ob. 2, Vn. 1, Vn. 2, Va., S, A, T, B, B.c. Source part names are "Hautb.", "Violini".

2. Quia respexit

Source layout is two four-stave systems per page: Ob. 1 solo, Ob. 2 solo, S solo, Vn. 1 / Vn. 2 / Va. Source part names are "Hautb. Soli", "Soprano Solo", "Violini e violette senza organo e Bassi".

3. Fecit potentiam

Source layout is one ten-stave system per page: Vn. 1, Vn. 2, Va., S, A, T, B, B.c., Ob. 1, Ob. 2. On the first page, oboe parts are notated in empty vocal staves; thereafter, they appear at the bottom of each page. Source part names are "Violini", "Hautbois".

4. Suscepit Israel

Source layout is two five-stave systems per page: Fl. 1 / Ob. 1 / Vn. 1, Fl. 2 / Ob. 2 / Vn. 2, Va., A solo, B.c. Source part name is "A.S."

5. Gloria

Source layout is one eight-stave system per page: Ob. 1 / Vn. 1, Ob. 2 / Vn. 2, Va., S, A, T, B, B.c. There are no source part names.

6. Sicut erat in principio

Source layout is one eight-stave system per page: Ob. 1 / Ob. 2 / Vn. 1, Vn. 2, Va., S, A, T, B, B.c. Source part names are "V.i. Hautb. i.2.", "Viol.2".

Magnificat in B-flat

D-Dlb Mus. 2398-D-25, size 310 x 225 mm., bound in four gatherings of two bifolia plus one bifolio (thirty-six pages). The first page is a title page and contains the text: "Magnificat 8^{vum} / à 5 Voci, Sop. A. T. 2 Bassi / con Flaut. Travers / VV. Haut.s. / di Giov. Heinichen / Mens Maij 1728". The setting is in five movements: "Magnificat," pages 2–7; "Quia respexit," pages 8–15; "Fecit potentiam," pages 16–23; "Suscepit Israel," pages 24–26; and "Gloria," pages 27–34. All pages are numbered and ruled with ten staves. The date "Mens Maij 1728" is at the bottom right of page 34. Measure number counts appear at the end of each movement.

1. Magnificat

Source layout is one eight-stave system per page: Ob. 1 / Vn. 1, Ob. 2 / Vn. 2, Va., S, A, T, B, B.c. There are no source part names.

2. Quia respexit

Source layout is one nine-stave system per page: Fl. 1, Fl. 2, Ob. 1, Ob. 2, Vn. 1, Vn. 2, Va., A solo, B.c. Source part names are "Flaut. Travers.", "Hautb. Con sordini", "V.V sempre piano", "A.S."

3. Fecit potentiam

Source layout on first page is one eleven-stave system, followed by ten-stave systems thereafter: Ob. 1 / Ob. 2 / Vn. 1 / Vn. 2 (oboes shown separately on page 1), Va., S, A, T, B, B solo 1, B solo 2, Bn. 1 / Bn. 2, B.c. Source part names are "Hautb", "V.V.", "Coro", "Basso i. concertato", "Basso 2 concertato", "2 Bassoni concertati".

4. Suscepit Israel

Source layout is two five-stave systems per page: Fl. 1 / Fl. 2, Vn. 1 / Vn. 2, Va., T solo, Vc. Source part names are "Flauti Trav.", "VV con sordini", "T.S.", "Violoncello senza organo".

5. Gloria

Source layout is one eight-stave system per page: Ob. 1 / Vn. 1, Ob. 2 / Vn. 2, Va., S, A, T, B, B.c. There are no source part names.

Ave maris stella

D-Dlb Mus. 2398-E-8, size 308 x 264 mm, bound in one gathering of three bifolia (twelve pages). The first page contains the title text: "Hymnus: Ave Maris Stella à 4 Voc. di Giov. Heinichen". There is crossed out text above and to the right of the title. The pages are numbered and ruled with twelve staves. The setting is in a single movement on pages 1–10. The word "Finis", a timing ("3 M"), and the date "Mens. 9br 1723" appear at the right of page 10.

Source layout is two five-stave systems per page: S / Vn. 1, A / Vn. 2, T / Va., B, B.c. Source part names are "Senza Hautbois", "Violino 1 col Soprano", "Violin. 2 con ContraAlto", "Violetta con Tenore".

Jesu Redemptor omnium

D-Dlb Mus. 2398-E-7, size 315 x 230 mm, bound in one gathering of two bifolia plus one bifolio (twelve pages). The first page contains the title text: "Hymnus in Nativitate domini à 4. Voc. di Giov. Heinichen". The pages are numbered and ruled with ten staves. The setting is in a single movement on pages 1–10, and the date "Mes. Xbr. 1724" is at the end of page 10.

Source layout is two five-stave systems per page: S / Ob. 1 / Vn. 1, A / Ob. 2 / Vn. 2, T / Va., B, B.c. Source part names are "Violin.i. col Soprano", "Viol.2. col ContraAlto", "Violetta col Tenore".

Alma Redemptoris Mater

Non-autograph source *D-Dlb* Mus. 2398-E-1, size 315 x 220 mm, bound in one gathering of three bifolia (twelve pages). The first page contains the title text: "Alma Redemptoris Di Giov: Heinichen". The pages are numbered and ruled with twelve staves. The setting is in a single movement on pages 1–11. The word "Fine" appears at the bottom right of page 11.

Source layout is one eleven-stave system per page: Ob. 1, Ob. 2, Vn. 1, Vn. 2, Va., S, A, T, B, B.c., Bn. Source part names are "Oboè", "VV^{ni}", "Viola", "Sopr:", "Alto:", "Ten:", "Basso:", "Fagotti".

Ave Regina

D-Dlb Mus. 2398-E-6, size 310 x 230 mm, bound in two gatherings of two bifolia (sixteen pages). The first page contains the title text: "Ave Regina à 2. Voci con Stromenti di Giov. Heinichen". The pages are numbered up to page 14 and ruled with ten staves. The setting is in three movements: "Ave Regina," pages 1–3; "Gaude Virgo gloriosa," pages 3–7; and "Vale," pages 7–13. A timing ("7M"), a measure count, and the date "Mens. Martij 1727" appear at the bottom right of page 13.

1. Ave Regina

Source layout is two five-stave systems per page: Fl. 1 / Ob. 1 / Vn. 1, Fl. 2 / Ob. 2 / Vn. 2, Va., A solo, B.c. Source part names are "Violini, Hautb. e Flaut. Traversieri", "Alto Solo".

2. Gaude Virgo gloriosa

Source layout is two five-stave systems per page: Ob. 1 / Ob. 2, Vn. 1 / Vn. 2, Va., S solo, B.c. Source part names are "Hautbois / 1.2.", "Viol: unis", "Soprano Solo".

3. Vale

Source layout on first page is one six-stave system: Fl. 1 / Fl. 2, Ob. 1 / Ob. 2, Vn. 1 / Vn. 2, Va., S solo, A solo, B.c.; second and subsequent pages have one eight-stave system per page: Fl. 1, Fl. 2, Ob. 1 / Vn. 1, Ob. 2 / Vn. 2, Va., S solo, A solo, B.c. Source part names are "Flauti Travers.", "Violini e Hautb. / Sempre piano", "Violetta", "Soprano", "ContraAlto".

Regina caeli in G

D-Dlb Mus. 2398-E-3, size 316 x 227 mm, bound in three gatherings of two bifolia (twenty-four pages). The first page contains the title text: "Regina Caeli à 4 Voc. con Strom. di Giov. Heinichen". The pages are numbered and ruled with ten staves. The setting is in four movements: "Regina caeli," pages 1–9; "Quia quem meruisti," pages 10–13; "Ora pro nobis," pages 14–16; and "Alleluia," pages 19–22. A measure number count appears at the end of each movement, and the date "Finis / Mens. / Martij / 1727" is at the bottom right of page 22.

1. Regina caeli

Source layout is one ten-stave system per page: Fl. 1, Fl. 2, Ob. 1 / Vn. 1, Ob. 2 / Vn. 2, Va., S, A, T, B, B.c. Source part name is "Fl. / Trav".

2. Quia quem meruisti

Source layout is two five-stave systems per page: Ob. 1, Ob. 2 / Ob. 3, Bn., T solo / Vn. 1 / Vn. 2, B.c. Source part names are "3 Hautb. / con / sordini", "Bassoni / con / sordini", "Tenore Solo / con I Violini / all'ottava alta, / sempre piano".

3. Ora pro nobis

Source layout is two five-stave systems per page: Fl. 1 / Fl. 2, Vn. 1 / Vn. 2 / Va., S solo, A solo, B.c. Original layout at start of movement and crossed out: Fl. 1, Fl. 2, S solo, A solo, Vn. 1 / Vn. 2 / Va. / B.c. Source part names are "Flauti trav", "Violini e Violette sempre piano", "à 2" (between the two vocal lines).

4. Alleluia

Source layout is one eight-stave system per page: Ob. 1 / Vn. 1, Ob. 2 / Vn. 2, Va., S, A, T, B, B.c. There are no source part names.

Regina caeli in D

D-Dlb Mus. 2398-E-4, size 310 x 265 mm, bound in probably three gatherings of two bifolia plus one bifolio (twenty-eight pages). The binding is very fragile and the spine is damaged. The first page contains the title text: "Regina Caeli Laetare". The pages are numbered and ruled with thirteen staves. The setting is in five movements: "Regina caeli," pages 1–8; "Quia quem meruisti," pages 8–14; "Resurrexit sicut dixit," pages 15–17; "Ora pro nobis," pages 18–19; and "Alleluia," pages 19–26. The word "Finis" appears at the bottom right of page 26.

1. Regina caeli

Source layout is one nine-stave system per page: Ob. 1 / Vn. 1, Ob. 2 / Vn. 2, Va., S, A solo, A, T, B, B.c. Source part names are "A Concertato", "A ripieno".

2. Quia quem meruisti

Source layout is one eight-stave system per page: Ob. 1 / Ob. 2 / Vn. 1, Vn. 2, Va., S, A, T, B, B.c. There are no source part names.

3. Resurrexit sicut dixit

Source layout is three four-stave systems per page: Ob. 1 / Ob. 2 / Vn. 1 / Vn. 2, Va., T solo, B.c. Source part name is "Tenore / Solo".

4. Ora pro nobis

Source layout is one eight-stave system per page: Ob. 1 / Vn. 1, Ob. 2 / Vn. 2, Va., S, A, T, B, B.c. Source part name is "Basso".

5. Alleluia

Source layout is one nine-stave system per page: Ob. 1 / Vn. 1, Ob. 2 / Vn. 2, Va., S, A solo, A, T, B, B.c. Source part names are "A. Conc.", "A. Rip."

Editorial Methods

Titles and Order of Works

All settings are given titles as per the *Liber Usualis*. They are grouped by genre (psalms, Magnificats, hymns, and antiphons), and presented alphabetically within each genre. Works with the same title are differentiated by key (e.g., *Magnificat in G*). Individual movements in multi-movement settings are given titles according to the text incipit and are numbered editorially. Additional information in the titles of the original sources—such as "Magnificat (6tum) à 4 Voc. Con strom"—is recorded in the section on sources above.

Score Order and General Notational Issues

The score order of the original source has been preserved except as follows. For clarity, source instrumental and vocal groupings of the original have been expanded. Thus, strictly *colla parte* settings of voices and instruments (e.g., soprano and violin 1) are divided, and oboe parts that differ in detail from violin parts are expanded onto separate staves at the top of the score. Also, the alto solo part embedded within the chorus in movements 1 and 5 of *Regina caeli in D* has been given its own staff to better set it apart, as seen in other works with a single solo voice. Finally, the single source basso continuo line is expanded into two lines, labelled "Basso ripieno" and "Basso continuo," to indicate where certain instruments drop in and out of the texture (see the introduction under "Notes on Performance").

Oboes were an expected part of the orchestral ensemble in Dresden, even when not specifically mentioned in the source (again, see the section on performance). Therefore, oboe parts have been added editorially where necessary.

Instrument names and abbreviations are given in English and are in brackets when supplied editorially. The addition of instrument names is somewhat haphazard in the sources and often in non-standard form (e.g., "violetta" for viola); where these are present, they are noted above in the section on sources. The original key of horns in the source is maintained but stated in English ("in D").

Tempo and other written directives meant to apply to the entire score are placed above the top staff and repeated above the vocal staves. Occasionally, different source directives are given for different groups of instruments; these are reflected in the transcription and are discussed in the critical notes as necessary.

All final barlines are modernized to thin-thick barlines, and source sectional divisions of thin-thin barlines are retained. The soprano, alto, and tenor voices use C1, C3, and C4 clefs, respectively, in the sources; these are modernized in the edition. Multiple occurrences of the same pitch class in key signatures are removed without comment, but otherwise source key signatures are retained. Meter signatures are modernized with respect to placement but are otherwise unaltered.

Notes and Rests

Original note values are retained, with the exception that in the two hymns, final breves are set as two tied semibreves. The stem directions, beamings, and rhythmic groupings of notes and rests in the source are made to conform to modern conventions in the edition. The notation of appoggiaturas is also modernized, that is, with stems up, although slurs are not added. Shorthand methods of notation, including *colla parte* indications, are written out, and any necessary clef adjustments made, without comment. Any resultant notes out of range are corrected and given in parentheses in the edition. Triplet numerals are placed at the beam or stem side of notes and are removed once a pattern is established. In *Alma Redemptoris Mater*, the parts of oboe 1, oboe 2, and bassoon, as well as notes in the final measure of the work in all sounding parts, were added later (exact date unknown) in a hand other than Heinichen's; these are optional in performance and have been set in a smaller size in the edition.

Expressive Markings, Dynamics, and Fermatas

The spelling, orthography, and placement of expressive and dynamic markings for individual parts are regularized. Fermatas are placed above staves. Any added markings or fermatas are placed in brackets. Fermatas of the source that occur only in vocal parts at the end of a phrase are indications that the singer's involvement in that particular movement has ended, and these are removed and reported in the critical notes; where a general pause is called for, fermatas are added in brackets as needed. Added letter dynamics are set in bold type, rather than the usual bold-italic; however, dynamics added as result of expanding *colla parte* notational shorthand are added without comment. Dynamics are rarely added in the horn and continuo parts, given their rarity in these parts in the sources.

Ornaments, Articulations, Slurs, and Ties

Ornaments and articulations are regularized with respect to placement. Ornaments added (as called for by parallel passages, for instance) are placed in brackets; added articulations (such as staccato markings) are placed in parentheses. The placement of slurs and ties is also regularized, though these are dashed when added. The practice of placing a dot after a barline to indicate a tied note is tacitly realized.

Accidentals

The modern convention that an accidental remains in effect throughout a measure unless cancelled has been adopted in this edition. Thus accidentals of the source that are made redundant by this convention are tacitly removed, while accidentals that become necessary because of this convention (e.g., a natural sign needed to cancel a previous sharp or flat) are tacitly added. Repeating accidentals required after a barline are also tacitly added. Other added accidentals are placed in brackets. Added cautionary accidentals are placed in parentheses; source cautionaries are retained.

Figured Bass

Figured bass symbols are placed above the bass staff in the edition. The sources are figured very sparsely (except the non-autograph setting of *Alma Redemptoris Mater*), and figures are usually below the staff. Editorial figures and symbols are enclosed in brackets. Inflections of intervals are regularized to precede the numeral, as in ♯6 (rather than 6♯).

Text Underlay

In the vocal parts, the spelling and orthography of the text underlay are regularized according to the *Liber Usualis*, except where the occasional idiosyncratic usage results in text of a different number of syllables from the *Liber Usualis*, in which case it is retained. Word divisions follow modern conventions. Punctuation is added as called for by repeated phrases. Text omitted as notational shorthand is added editorially without comment, as in no case does any ambiguity arise. Other editorially added text is placed in square brackets. The text underlay of the source is at times fairly inexact; it is neatened without comment. In no case is there any doubt as to the underlay required.

Critical Notes

The notes below always describe rejected source readings, apart from instances where retained text deviations from the *Liber Usualis* are described. Pitch names are standard: c' refers to middle C. The following abbreviations are used: M(m). = measures(s), Fl. = Flute, Ob. = Oboe, Vn. = Violin, Va. = Viola, S = Soprano, A = Alto, T = Tenor, B = Bass, Bn. = Bassoon, Vc. = Violoncello, B.r. = Basso ripieno, B.c. = Basso continuo

Beatus vir

M. 94, A solo and T solo, note has fermata.

Confitebor tibi Domine

M. 1, B.c., note 1, "Senza Bassi Ripieni" indication. M. 5, B.c., note 1, "Tutti li Bassi" indication. M. 72, B.c., note 3, "Senza Bassi Ripieni" indication. M. 77, B.c., note 1, "Tutti li Bassi" indication.

Dixit Dominus

M. 35, Ob. 2, note 1 is c'. Mm. 38–39, B.c., source is illegible.

In exitu Israel

1. IN EXITU ISRAEL

Bass clef is used in Vn. 1, Vn. 2, Va., except for m. 28, note 2 through m. 31, and m. 44 through m. 47. M. 27, Vn. 1, Vn. 2, Va., Vc., note 7 lacks ♮. M. 42, Vn. 1, Vn. 2, Va., Vc., notes 3 and 15 lack ♮. M. 43, Vn. 1, Vn. 2, Va., Vc., note 7 lacks ♮.

2. NON NOBIS DOMINE

M. 11, *Liber Usualis* has "veritate"—source "verite" is retained to preserve number of syllables. M. 14, A solo, *Liber Usualis* has "nequando"—source "quando" is retained to preserve number of syllables.

4. DOMUS ISRAEL

Tempo above B.c. staff is *Allegro*, while tempo above Vn. 1 staff is *Vivace*; the edition uses *Allegro (Vivace)*. Mm. 34–35, S solo, *Liber Usualis* has "Domino"—source "eum" is retained to preserve number of syllables. M. 92, T solo, note has fermata.

Laetatus sum

M. 45, B.c., note 3 is C♯.   M. 168, A solo, notes 6–7 are 16th notes.   M. 179, A solo and T solo, note has fermata.

Lauda Jerusalem

Mm. 36–37, *Liber Usualis* has "nebulam"—source "nubeculam" is retained to preserve number of syllables.

Laudate pueri

M. 34, Ob. 2, Vn. 2, note 5 lacks ♯.

Magnificat in G

2. Quia respexit

Performance indication above Ob. solo 1 staff is *Andante e dolcemente sempre,* while indication above Vn. 1, 2 staff is *Andante e sempre pianissimo;* the edition uses *Andante* for the tempo and places the other instructions as shown.

3. Fecit potentiam

M. 33, B.c., note 2, "Bassi ripieni" indication.

Magnificat in B-flat

1. Magnificat

Mm. 19–29, S set as single staff; m. 23 repeats the "solo" indication.

3. Fecit potentiam

M. 13, Bn. solo 1, Bn. solo 2, B.r., B.c., note 10 lacks ♭.

Alma Redemptoris Mater

M. 1, A has "à 4tro soli"; moved above S staff in edition.   M. 4, Ob. 1, S, note 2 (appoggiatura) lacks ♭.   M. 6, T, note 2 (appoggiatura) lacks ♭.   M. 19, Ob. 1, note 7 is c″.   M. 22, A has "soli" indication, referring to all four vocal parts; in the edition, rather than "soli" being used for all four parts, "solo" is used for each part individually, as seen in the source in mm. 4–7.   M. 36, T, notes 1–2 are 8th notes.   M. 44, S has "soli," referring to the four vocal parts; as before, "solo" is used in the edition for each part individually.

Ave Regina

1. Ave Regina

Mm. 10–11, A solo, text is "exorta."   M. 17, A solo, note 8 is dotted.   M. 18, A solo, note 4 is dotted.   Mm. 18–20, A solo, text is "exorta."   Mm. 22–23, A solo, text is "exorta."

2. Gaude Virgo gloriosa

M. 38, S solo, note 3 has fermata.

3. Vale

M. 52, A solo, note is c′.   M. 58, S solo and A solo, note has fermata.

Regina caeli in G

1. Regina caeli

M. 11, Fl. 2, one quarter rest missing.   M. 23, Vn. 2, note 4 lacks ♯.

2. Quia quem meruisti

M. 21, T, solo, note missing.   M. 43, T solo, note missing.

Regina caeli in D

1. Regina caeli

M. 37, A solo, note has fermata.   M. 41, B, text is "portaluia."

3. Resurrexit sicut dixit

M. 49, Va., note 1 is 8th note.   M. 57, T solo, note has fermata.